Dyslexia: Sur
succeeding a

Dyslexia: Surviving and Succeeding at College is a practical and easy-to-read guide for dyslexic and dyspraxic students. Clearly and simply written, in a dyslexia-friendly format, it addresses not just study skills but also more general aspects of coping with student life.

Each chapter includes step-by-step strategies which can be put into practice from the very first day at college. You will learn how to:

- read accurately and quickly with good comprehension;
- take notes efficiently from books and in lectures;
- contribute confidently in seminars;
- develop memory strategies for study and everyday life;
- organise your time and plan your work.

Sylvia Moody recognises that adapting to student life generally is as important as developing study skills. Guidance is given to assist you in finding your way around campus, building relationships with tutors, managing emotional development and preparing for the world of work. Full of invaluable self-help strategies, this book will empower you to improve your skills in all areas.

The book will also be useful to subject tutors who wish to learn about dyslexia, and to dyslexia tutors and coordinators who want to give practical advice to their students.

Sylvia Moody is a freelance writer and psychologist specialising in adult dyslexia.

Dyslexia: Surviving and succeeding at college

Sylvia Moody

Routledge
Taylor & Francis Group

LONDON AND NEW YORK

First published 2007
by Routledge
2 Park Square, Milton Park, Abingdon, Oxon OX14 4RN

Simultaneously published in the USA and Canada
by Routledge
711 Third Avenue, New York, NY 10017

*Routledge is an imprint of the Taylor & Francis Group,
an informa business*

© 2007 Sylvia Moody

Typeset in Century Schoolbook, Tekton and Gill by
BC Typesetting Ltd, Bristol

British Library Cataloguing in Publication Data
A catalogue record for this book is available from the British
Library

Library of Congress Cataloging in Publication Data
Moody, Sylvia, 1941–
    Dyslexia: surviving and succeeding at college/Sylvia Moody.
       p.   cm.
    Includes index.
    ISBN 978–0–415–43058–6 (hardback: alk. paper) –
    ISBN 978–0–415–43059–3 (pbk.: alk. paper)
    1. Dyslexia. 2. Dyslexics–Education (Higher) 3. Study skills.
    4. Self-help techniques. I. Title.
    LB1050.5.M665 2007
    371.91′44–dc22
    2006036690

ISBN10: 0–415–43058–5 (hbk)
ISBN10: 0–415–43059–3 (pbk)
ISBN10: 0–203–96130–7 (ebk)

ISBN13: 978–0–415–43058–6 (hbk)
ISBN13: 978–0–415–43059–3 (pbk)
ISBN13: 978–0–203–96130–8 (ebk)

Contents

Preface

If you are a student with dyslexic or dyspraxic difficulties, you will know that college life presents you with a number of challenges: reading lists that rear up like impassable mountain ranges, essays that turn into uncontrollable writhing monsters, lectures that fall through bottomless chasms in your memory and seminars where your tongue seems to have unaccountably tied itself into a knot. Well . . . perhaps your difficulties aren't quite that dramatic, but if you do have difficulties at college of whatever type or severity, I hope that this book will provide helpful guidance and advice.

In Part I of the book, I shall describe dyslexic and dyspraxic difficulties and show how they affect different aspects of study. I shall also explain what sort of help is available to you and what are the procedures in further education, higher education and professional training courses for accessing that help.

In Part II, I'll give advice on quick and practical ways to develop and improve your study skills. Particular topics covered are organisational skills, reading accurately with good comprehension, note-taking, academic writing, memory strategies, seminar presentations, examination techniques and research skills. There is also advice from a dyslexic student on how to deal with the emotional 'side effects' of dyslexia.

Part III of the book includes a quick guide to dyslexia for subject tutors and advice on how to manage dyslexia when you move on from college into the workplace.

In the final part of the book, you will find checklists, advice on IT support, a list of help organisations and suggestions for further reading.

You may be aware that some of your friends, even if not dyslexic, have difficulties with various aspects of study skills. If so, you might like to show them Part II of this book, as it may be of use to them. All students need good study skills; it's just that dyslexic students need them more than most.

I hope that you enjoy reading the book, and that you will find it helpful.

Sylvia Moody
Dyslexia Assessment Service
London

Acknowledgements

In writing this book I have greatly benefited from the advice and support of my colleagues Diana Bartlett, Susan Close, Jean Jameson, Katherine Kindersley and Anne Kingston.

Part I

Dyslexia at college

Introduction

In the first chapter of this section, Clare, a dyslexic student, describes the difficulties she experienced at the beginning of her university course and how she eventually overcame them.

In the two following chapters, I explain the range and nature of dyslexic and dyspraxic difficulties and the way in which these difficulties relate to particular study problems. I also give advice about the sort of help and support you will need at college and how to go about getting it.

Chapter 1

A cautionary tale

Hello, I'm Clare – I'm just coming to the end of a three-year psychology degree, and I've been asked to write a few words about how I've coped with my dyslexia at college.

The first thing to say is that I've known ever since I can remember that I have dyslexic difficulties. I was assessed very early on at school and had some help and got extra time in examinations. By the time I reached the sixth form, I felt I was coping quite well with my difficulties and didn't feel they hampered me too much. In fact, I tended to concentrate more on the positive sides of being dyslexic, like understanding things intuitively and being good at lateral thinking.

Anyway, when I got accepted at London University for a psychology degree, I just assumed I'd cope somehow. So I had a carefree gap year, travelling, working in the local wine bar and ignoring my parents' advice to do some preliminary reading for my course.

When I arrived at college, I was pleased to find that my hall of residence was close to the main campus. So the first thing I did was to go out to explore – and the second thing I did was to get completely lost. I don't have much sense of direction, and the buildings all seemed to look the same. I'd been given a map, but I had a problem understanding it. An annoying thing was that, even when I managed to find places, like the library, I would then lose them again.

After a week or so, I sort of got my bearings, and on the day that the first seminar was scheduled, I actually managed to find my way to the seminar room, at the right time, and to have the right books with me. It seemed like a good start.

There were about twelve of us at the seminar, and the subject was neuro-psychology, a word I didn't really understand and could hardly pronounce. Anyway, it turned out to be about how the brain is wired up and which parts of it do things like speaking and listening.

As the tutor talked about this subject, I began to think that the listening bit in *my* brain couldn't be working. The tutor kept explaining things, and other people were asking intelligent questions, but the whole thing seemed to be going right past me. I just wasn't taking in what the tutor said. The upshot was that, at the end of the seminar, I had no more idea about neuro-psychology than I had at the beginning. I felt foolish and sort of inadequate, but I didn't like to say that I hadn't really followed anything.

Before leaving, the tutor gave us a list of journal articles to read for the following week's seminar. She said the articles would make clear to us what brain processes were involved in the skill of reading. So the next day I went to the library and settled down to read the articles.

At this point it became clear to me that the bit in my brain that was 'involved in the skill of reading' had somehow also gone missing. As I read through the articles, I found I couldn't really understand them. A lot of the words were long and unfamiliar, and it seemed to take an eternity just to read one article. The bit of my brain that did memory was obviously missing too, because I couldn't remember anything about what I'd read. I sat in the library for hours that week trying to read the articles and getting more and more upset.

When the day of the next seminar came round, I felt a sense of dread. During the seminar, I was relieved that I wasn't asked to say anything. Most of the other students had plenty to say or questions to ask, and there was a lot of general discussion. I just sat there not saying anything and not really following anything. All I could think about was: Why is all this so difficult for me? What has gone wrong?

But worse was to come. At the end of the seminar, the tutor set us an essay on reading mechanisms in the brain and suggested yet more articles we might want to look at. I won't prolong the agony by trying to describe to you the torments I went through in trying to tackle this essay because 'some of the events described might be too distressing to my readers'. All I will say is that, at the end of my first month at college, I was not having the marvellous carefree time I had anticipated. I was, as often as not, sitting depressed or crying in my room, feeling completely exhausted and wondering whether there were any parts of my brain that were actually functioning.

Perhaps I would have given up and just gone off the course, but, fortunately, in this darkest hour, rescue came to me in the form of Deborah, the dyslexia support tutor. I unexpectedly received an e-mail from her suggesting that we meet to discuss any difficulties I might be experiencing. Deborah hadn't magically divined my despair; it's simply that I'd ticked the dyslexia box on my application form without thinking much about it, and now she was following this up in a routine way by contacting me.

My meeting with Deborah marked the moment when things began to change for the better. At first I was quite emotional, sobbing and saying that I wouldn't be able to cope. But Deborah calmed me down and assured me that lots of dyslexic students had major problems at the beginning of their course. She said she was sure I would cope once I got some help in place, and, meantime, she would let my tutors know I needed extra support. Basically, she said: just hold on, keep your nerve, things will get better.

She was right. I didn't turn overnight into super-student, but I felt that I could see some way forward, some prospect of things improving, of not being alone with my problems.

Looking back, I've asked myself how it was that everything went so horribly wrong in those first few weeks. With hindsight, I think it was a combination of things. It would have been good if I'd followed my parents' advice and had done a bit of preliminary reading during my gap year. I hadn't done psychology for A-level, so all the vocabulary used was unfamiliar to me. I think a second problem was that when things did go wrong I didn't ask anyone for help – I just went on trying to deal with the situation myself, perhaps thinking that, if I couldn't, I was a failure. I think I also got quite frightened by the thought that I might actually not be able to continue the course. I didn't have a Plan B.

Also, if I'm honest, I have to admit that it could have been partly the fact that I had been a little bit arrogant. I'd always prided myself on coping well at school, and I just assumed – wrongly as it turned out – that I'd easily be able to cope at university too. I just hadn't anticipated how much more reading there would be, how much more pressure I would be under to do things quickly. Hindsight, as they say, is a great thing.

Anyway, I did cope in the end, thanks to all the support I received and, of course, through my own hard work. I did have to put in longer hours than most of my friends. The pay-off was that, by the second term, I had begun to actually enjoy my course, and now I feel it's the best thing I've ever done. In fact, I've turned into an eternal student: I'm planning to go on to do a postgraduate course in neuro-psychology!

Chapter 2

Dyslexia and dyspraxia

In this chapter, I shall describe dyslexic difficulties and show how these overlap with a related set of difficulties, known as dyspraxia. I shall then explain how both dyslexic and dyspraxic difficulties cause particular problems with study skills. The chapter ends with a description of the talents and strengths which many dyslexic and dyspraxic people possess and which provide a valuable counterweight to their difficulties.

Dyslexia and dyspraxia explained

Most people feel that they cope well with some things but are hopeless at others. One person may struggle to write a letter but be easily able to build a house. Another person may be an academic high-flyer but socially inept. Yet another may be a gifted artist but unable to read a book.

People who have dyslexic or dyspraxic difficulties tend to be inefficient in particular ways, and these areas of weakness can be shown on a continuum (see Figure 2.1). (All the terms used in the figure will be explained in detail below.)

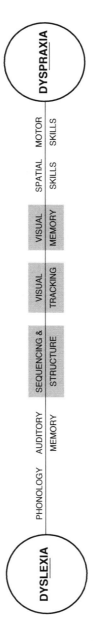

Figure 2.1 The dyslexia–dyspraxia continuum.

A person described as dyslexic would certainly have weaknesses in phonology and auditory memory. They would probably also have difficulty with the middle three areas shown with shading, but not necessarily with spatial and motor skills.

A person described as dyspraxic would certainly have weaknesses in spatial and motor skills. They would probably also have difficulty with the middle three shaded areas, but not necessarily with auditory memory or phonology.

So, everyone has a different mix of difficulties, and the purpose of an assessment is to establish each person's pattern of strengths and weaknesses.

Phonology

Phonology means the ability to recognise, pronounce, blend, separate and sequence the sounds of a language. So, people with poor phonological skills make mistakes in reading, spelling and pronouncing words (especially long words) and find it hard to read quickly or to read out loud.

Auditory memory

Auditory memory affects almost everything we do in life: thinking, speaking, writing, listening, remembering. In study, the following difficulties are common:

- following lectures, discussions and conversations;
- keeping track of your ideas when speaking to other people;
- remembering instructions and directions;
- concentrating for long periods;
- remembering names;
- remembering formulae;
- multitasking, e.g., listening and taking notes.

Sequencing and structure

Sequencing and structure help us to organise our lives in a logical and efficient way. We use them when we have a conversation, write a letter or an essay, listen to a lecture or plan our day. In fact, almost everything we do is structured in some way. Perhaps the only time we are not imprisoned within structures is when we are dreaming. So, difficulty with sequencing and structure affects the following:

- organising a work schedule;
- planning ahead;
- structuring ideas in oral presentations;
- structuring an essay;
- understanding written text;
- carrying out instructions in the correct order;
- filing documents and locating filed documents;
- looking up entries in directories and dictionaries;
- carrying out tasks in an efficient logical way.

Visual tracking

Visual tracking is a skill you use when you visually analyse a set of symbols. This could be a line of letters, or a line of numbers, or a more complicated visual image, such as a formula or equation, or a table of figures. So, poor visual tracking will cause problems in these areas:

- writing or copying numbers correctly;
- keeping numbers in columns;
- seeing the correct sequence of letters in a word;
- keeping your place on the page when reading;
- analysing maps, graphs, charts, tables of figures;
- reading complicated formulae or equations;
- setting out work neatly.

VISUAL STRESS

Some people report that they find it visually stressful to look at lines of print or dense patterns of any kind. They say that print seems to 'jump about' and that lines blur. They also find that white paper 'glares'. Problems of this type are known as visual stress.

Visual stress is not part of a dyslexic syndrome but is often associated with dyslexia and adds an extra difficulty to reading.

For more information on this, see page 21, and pages 64–5.

Visual memory

Poor visual memory causes problems with spelling irregular words; remembering material presented visually, e.g., mind maps; remembering where you have put things; and remembering where particular buildings are and which route you take to reach them.

Spatial skills

Spatial skills are required in any situation in which you have to judge distance, space or direction. Examples would be throwing a ball to someone, parking a car and telling left from right.

It may surprise you that spatial skills are also important in social situations. When you are with a friend, or at a social gathering, you need to judge the amount of 'social space' you need to leave between you and the person you're speaking to. Dyspraxic people often report difficulty with this: they feel that they often talk too much or too loudly, that they tend to interrupt people and that generally they are not good team players.

Poor spatial skills are also often associated with poor judgement of time. This is not surprising given that we tend to see time as stretching out before us like space and, indeed, use phrases like 'length of time', 'a long stretch'.

Motor skills

The term 'motor skills' means the skills we use when we plan and carry out physical movements. There are two types of motor skills: fine motor skills and gross motor skills.

We use fine motor skills for 'small-scale' tasks such as:

- handwriting;
- presenting written work neatly;
- using a word processor, calculator or telephone keypad;
- doing any task that requires good manual skill, e.g., woodwork, needlework;
- using laboratory equipment or scientific instruments.

We use gross motor skills for 'large-scale' tasks, such as playing sports or driving a car.

Poor motor control is *the* characteristic feature of dyspraxia. In addition to the problems mentioned above, dyspraxic people often have difficulties with balance: they tend to trip up or bump into things. They are also prone to spilling and dropping things.

Dyslexia and dyspraxia checklists
can be found in
Appendix A.
These cover both study and everyday difficulties.

Positive aspects of dyslexia and dyspraxia

People vary in the way they feel about their dyslexia (or dyspraxia). Some regard it as, at best, a nuisance, at worst a major handicap; others feel it confers benefits. In general, people whose difficulties have been recognised at an early stage, and who have received appropriate help, develop a positive attitude. They have good strategies in place to deal with the difficulties, and their energy is therefore free to flow into creative channels.

In the previous chapter, Clare mentioned that, when she was at school, she was very positive about her dyslexia, as she felt that in many ways it was a source of strength. After she got past her first difficult term at college, she continued to develop, and to capitalise on, her particular talents, which she describes as follows:

I feel that, because I'm not too good at logical thinking, I'm able to think about things in a holistic and creative way. I'm often quicker than other people in seeing links and associations between things and in knowing what needs to be done in a situation. I feel I'm quite enterprising – I'm good at problem-solving because I can think laterally, 'outside the box'.

Also, I think I'm quite intuitive and empathic. Because a lot of things are difficult for me, I'm sympathetic to other people who have difficulties of any kind, and try to think of ways to help them. I'm very practical and very determined, and I'm prepared to work hard to achieve my ambitions.

So Clare was able to strike a good balance between her strengths and difficulties and to stay on good terms with her dyslexia.

In the next chapter, I shall explain how you can access help and support for your difficulties when you are at college; and in Part II of the book, I shall suggest strategies which you yourself can use to deal with all the types of difficulty discussed in this chapter.

PROBLEMS AND SOLUTIONS

Joanna, music student
I have difficulty learning and understanding songs in foreign languages. I've solved the problem by getting a PDA. It can store songs and also translator packages for all the major European languages.

Ahmed, social-science student
I have trouble keeping my place when I'm looking at complicated tables of data or statistics.

I find it helps a lot to use an eye-level coloured reading ruler and also to highlight chunks of numbers in different colours.

Gerry, trainee nurse
I'm quite slow in getting my thoughts together to say something and don't always contribute as well as I would like in clinical case conferences.

Recently I summoned up the courage to speak to my supervisor about this. Since then, he and the rest of the group have encouraged me to speak out at meetings, and I've got more confident with practice.

Chapter 3

Accessing help and support

As a dyslexic student, you are entitled to receive help and support for your study difficulties and to request concessions, such as extra time, in examinations. In this chapter, I shall describe various types of help and support which may be useful to you, how to access these and how to go about applying for the Disabled Students Allowance.

Help and support

The help and support available to you could include:

1   dyslexia tuition;
2   IT support/technological aids;
3   optometry (for visual stress);
4   occupational therapy (for dyspraxia);
5   social skills;
6   general counselling;
7   concessions for course work and examinations.

Tuition

You will probably be allocated an individual dyslexia tutor or be given a list of tutors to contact yourself; and you may also have the opportunity to attend a study-skills group. The tuition should cover every aspect of your dyslexic difficulties. If you are dyspraxic, then the tuition would cover the educational aspects of dyspraxic difficulties but not problems with physical coordination. The latter would be treated by an occupational therapist (see below). So, a tuition programme should include some or all of the following.

Reading

Understanding and remembering what you read; summarising; improving speed and fluency; multi-sensory learning techniques; letter perception and tracking.

General writing skills

Training in clear, correct and coherent writing; spelling rules and word structure; grammar and punctuation; sentence construction and writing flow; paragraphing; proofreading.

Essay writing

Researching material; brainstorming for ideas; organisation and planning of contents; basic essay structure; ordering and linking of sections; signposting structure of essay to reader; essay writing for exams.

Study skills

Training in effective study and revision; organisation and presentation of material for easy learning; note-taking; summarising and highlighting.

Attention, concentration and memory

Exercises to focus and sustain attention and concentration; memory techniques.

Work organisation

Revision schedules and timetables; setting and achieving goals and sub-goals; meeting deadlines; efficient work methods; planning and organising tasks and projects; keeping in control of workload.

Oral communication

Presenting topics in seminars; contributing to discussions; dealing with word-retrieval problems.

Numeric and clerical skills

Accuracy and efficiency in basic figure work; data entry; copying and presentation; filing.

Attitude and interaction

Techniques to build up confidence and increase assertiveness; dealing with stress and reducing anxiety and frustration.

IT support/technological aids

There is a wide range of IT and technological support. For a detailed description of what is available, see Appendix B (p. 193). Below is a list of items which most dyslexic students find useful:

- personal computer;
- text-to-speech software to read documents, files or web pages and to read your essays back to you;
- mind-mapping software to help with the planning of flow charts, essays, laboratory reports, work schedules, etc.;
- voice recognition software to convert speech into text;
- PDA to help with work organisation;
- digital voice recorder to record lectures and discussions;
- hand-held spellchecker;

- screen-reading ruler;
- textic toolbar to choose colours on computer screen.

Optometry

If you suffer from visual stress (see pages 64–5), you may benefit from using:

- coloured overlays;
- an eye-level coloured reading ruler;
- a screen-reading ruler.

It may also be advisable to have a professional assessment done by an optometrist who specialises in colorimetry. The optometrist will be able to advise you on which coloured overlays are most helpful to you and which colour you should choose for your computer screen. Tinted lenses may be recommended.

Occupational therapy

If you are dyspraxic and have particular difficulties with physical coordination, you may benefit from help from an occupational therapist. Such therapists may be found through the college health centre or through your GP. *It is important to request a therapist who is experienced in dealing with adult development dyspraxia.*

Social skills

Your dyslexia tutor may be able to help you to improve your social skills. If not, enquire at the college health centre to see if they run a social-skills course or can recommend a trainer.

General counselling

If you have emotional difficulties, either connected to your dyslexia or more general in nature, you could request to see a counsellor at the college health centre, or you could contact a general counselling organisation (see p. 210).

Concessions

You should be able to request extra time and rest breaks in examinations. If you have difficulties with handwriting, you can request the use of a word processor or a scribe (typist) in your examinations. You can also ask for concessions for course work, e.g., you could ask for essay deadlines to be extended.

You will probably be able to request time extensions for library loans, and you may qualify for free photocopying facilities. You may also be eligible to use library computers which have preloaded assistive software.

You could also ask your tutors to give you extra help – for example, they could offer advice on focusing your reading, provide copies of lecture outlines in advance and take account of the fact that you might find difficulty with reading aloud or speaking out at seminars.

If your tutors seem uninformed about dyslexia, photocopy Chapter 11 of this book and give it to them. If you find it difficult to approach a tutor yourself, ask your dyslexia support coordinator to intercede for you.

How to access support

All educational establishments have a legal obligation to give appropriate support to dyslexic and dyspraxic students. However, the processes for accessing this support, and the sources of funding for it, are different in further education, higher education and professional training courses.

If you are at a further-education college or doing professional training, you can request all the types of help mentioned in the previous section, but the funding for these will probably come from the college itself and may be relatively limited.

Every college and training course is different, both in their awareness of dyslexia and in their preparedness to deal with it. In each case, you need to locate the appropriate member of staff – the disability officer, or the dyslexia support coordinator, or the student support officer – and get a clear idea of what help is available and how you can access it.

In higher education, there is a standard but more complicated procedure for applying for dyslexia support because the funding for this comes through a local-education-authority (LEA) grant called the Disabled Students Allowance (DSA). This Allowance, which is not means-tested, has the following components:

- specialist equipment allowance, e.g., for a computer;
- non-medical helpers allowance, e.g., for a tutor, reader, typist;
- a general allowance, which can be used for 'extras', such as photocopying and buying books;
- travel allowance.

Applying for the Disabled Students Allowance

Most UK students doing a first degree, either full-time or part-time, will be eligible for the DSA, and so will most postgraduate students. Applying for the Allowance is a relatively lengthy process, but *the dyslexia support coordinator at your college will be able to guide you through it*. The stages you will have to go through in your application are as follows.

Arrange a diagnostic assessment

The dyslexia support coordinator at your college will be able to give you a list of qualified assessors. You may have to pay for this assessment yourself, but often the college is willing to finance it.

If you have had a diagnostic dyslexia assessment since your sixteenth birthday, you may not be required to have another one at this stage. Check with the dyslexia support coordinator at your college.

Discuss your diagnostic assessment report with your dyslexia support coordinator

You need to be sure that you fully understand your diagnostic assessment report and the implications it may have for the academic, practical and fieldwork requirements of your course of study. Also, you need to be clear about exactly what help you will be requesting in the next stage of the application process, which is called the needs assessment.

Arrange a needs assessment

Apply to your LEA for a needs assessment, sending a copy of your diagnostic assessment report for approval. The LEA will fund this assessment and usually specifies a centre at which it will be carried out. You do not do any further tests in this assessment; you simply discuss your study needs (as specified in the diagnostic report) with the assessor. You will receive a report listing the equipment and tuition that the assessor will be recommending to your LEA.

Discuss your needs assessment report with your dyslexia support coordinator

If you, or the coordinator, feel that your needs have not been fully addressed in your needs assessment report, you can ask for appropriate revisions.

You have now completed the DSA application process. It can take several months to work through the above four stages of the process. So, if you make your initial application at the beginning of your first term, it will probably be your second term before you receive your DSA. However, most LEAs will be prepared to advance you some money for tuition or to agree to refund tuition fees retrospectively as soon as they have received, and approved, your diagnostic assessment report.

You don't need to wait until you are actually at college before making your initial application for a DSA. If possible, begin this process several months before you go up to college and have it completed by the time your first term begins. For this to happen, one of the following three things needs to be the case:

- You are prepared to pay for your own diagnostic assessment.
- Your college is prepared to pay for the assessment once they have made you a conditional or final offer of a place.
- You have had a diagnostic assessment in the past, and the LEA is prepared to accept the report from this assessment.

If you do arrange a diagnostic assessment before you go up to college, you need to be sure that the person who does your assessment has appropriate qualifications and experience of assessing adults in further and higher education. You could contact the dyslexia support unit at your local university, or at the university you will be attending, and ask them to recommend an assessor. Or you could contact the local branch of Dyslexia Action (see p. 203).

If you would like further advice on the help and support available to you at college and how to access this, contact SKILL (see p. 201) or the British Dyslexia Association (see p. 202). For a detailed guide to the DSA regulations, call the Department for Education and Skills helpline on 0800 731 9133 and request their information leaflet: 'Bridging the Gap: A Guide to the Disabled Student Allowances in Higher Education'.

Part II

Improving skills

Introduction

In this section of the book, I shall give practical advice on how to cope with your first weeks at college and how to develop efficient study skills. All areas of study are covered: scheduling work, time management, reading, note-taking, doing research, writing essays and laboratory reports, contributing to seminars, following instructions and taking examinations. Emotional aspects of dyslexia are also discussed.

Chapter 4

Getting organised

The first priority when you arrive at college is to get yourself organised. I'm going to suggest that you do this in three phases:

1   Explore your territory.
2   Learn to use tools.
3   Organise and plan activities.

I shall make some detailed suggestions for doing these three things below. Please note that you should aim to complete Phases 1 and 2 in the first week of your first term.

Exploring your territory

If you have ever owned a dog, you will know that, if you take it to a new place, the first thing this canny canine does is to prowl around and explore its new territory. It satisfies itself about the location of everything and makes itself comfortable in its new surroundings. When you first arrive at college, you need to do something similar: you need to become familiar with your surroundings, find out where everything is and be sure you know how to get from one place to another.

Probably you will have been given a map of the college buildings or campus. Your first task, before setting out to explore, is to study the map and get a rough idea of where the various college buildings are in relation to where you are located, and also in relation to each other. The map may be difficult to understand initially: it may show a confusing collection of buildings with their names written in small letters, or the buildings may just be numbered and you have to look up the numbers in a separate key.

So, begin by identifying those buildings which you are likely to want to visit and highlight them in colour on the map. For example, you'll want to know not just where the bar and the shop are, but also the whereabouts of the library and the lecture rooms or laboratories. It's important, too, to locate the office of the dyslexia support coordinator.

When you have located, on the map, the buildings which are of interest to you, set out, with the map, to walk around the campus and locate the actual buildings. On some campuses there can be rows of buildings which look very much alike. In such cases, take a careful note of particular landmarks which will help you to work out where you are. These could be, for example, a door painted in a particular colour, a tree or a pile of dustbins. You can add a note of the landmarks to your map.

When you find the library, go into it and ask at the desk for a library guide. Then familiarise yourself with the layout of the library. In particular, find out where your subject section is, where the journals are kept and where the general reference books are.

Also, find out where the photocopiers are located. Some may be in an obvious place, such as by the main library desk, but there could be others in odd corners of the building, which are less likely to be in use.

Make sure, when you leave the library, that you have with you a library guide with a note of the library opening hours, both in term time and in the holidays. The guide will probably include information on:

- the times of library induction tours;
- when the computer room is available;
- how far in advance you need to book a computer slot;
- whether, as a dyslexic student, you can book extra long sessions;
- whether some, or all, of the computers have dyslexia-friendly software.

Learning to use tools

In this second phase, you will learn how to use the various 'tools', or pieces of equipment, which are available to you. Using an evolutionary metaphor, you are now moving from the canine phase to the chimpanzee phase.

Library catalogue

It is very important that you don't wait until you get handed an essay topic and a reading list before finding out how to use the library catalogue, So, before you are under any pressure to produce an essay to a deadline, do a practice run in the library: search for a couple of books relevant to your subject.

You may have been able to join a guided tour of the library, in which case you will have been given instructions about how to find books in the computer catalogue. However, you may not have taken in everything the librarian said, so you probably need to spend some time reading through the instructions in the library guide and practising using the catalogue yourself.

Let's say that, for a practice run, you decide to find a book called *The Psychology of Reading* by John Stevens. The process of finding this book will involve several stages, each of which can present some difficulty to a dyslexic student:

Getting down the book reference correctly off the computer

References can be muddling jumbles of letters and numbers. For example, your computer search may throw up the following reference for your book:

M2-K735 Ste

Write the reference down clearly in largish letters, leaving a good space between the different parts of the reference:

M 2- K 735 Ste

Check the reference once.

Decoding the reference

Now that you've got the reference down correctly, what next? What does 'M2-K735 Ste' mean in terms of actually finding the book? You now need to consult your library guide again in order to decode the reference. From the guide, let's say you find that:

M   = main library
2   = Level 2
K   = Section K
735 = subject code
Ste = first three letters of author's name

Finding the relevant section of the library

First, you need to find your way to Level 2 in the main library building. As you will probably already be in the main building, this should be simple. If you need to find another building, consult the map in the library guide.

When you're on the right level in the right building, you need to search for Section K. This can be confusing. Very often libraries have series of book-shelves marked at the end with letters and numbers. There may be signs saying:

← A–I   → J–P

If you have difficulty with the alphabetic sequence, or if you tend to mix up letters, you could feel confused, even panicky. Is K to the left or the right? You can give yourself a bit of help in such situations by always carrying with you a small alphabet arc so that you can quickly check the letter sequence. Now you can see at a glance that K comes between J and P.

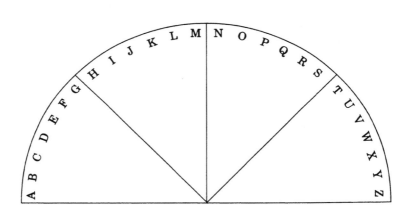

Finding the book

Now that you've found section K, you just need to concentrate on the last part of the reference:

735 Ste

The numbers 735 are the subject code, i.e., the code for all books on the subject of reading. There could be two or three shelves of books in Section K with this code. However, all the books marked 735 will be shelved in alphabetical order according to author, so you need to use your alphabet key again to find, first, the S authors and, within that group, the St authors, and then the Ste authors. You should be able to spot the Stevens book now.

Perhaps some of my readers will think that all this is very obvious. However, one of the main difficulties reported by dyslexic students is finding their way around library systems. As we saw above, there are things that can trip you up at every stage. The important thing is to keep calm and to work methodically through each of the stages. Of course, not all library systems will be exactly the same as the one I have described above, but the example I have used will give you the general principles of finding your way around a library.

Photocopiers

The next thing is to find out how the photocopiers work. You should have found out where they were located in Phase 1 of this exercise; now you need to know exactly how to use them. Do a couple of practice photocopies. Then find out how to do enlarged photocopies. If you have your campus map with you, you might like to do an enlarged copy of this.

Check if there is any coloured copying paper available for the use of dyslexic students. If not, you could ask the librarian about this or make a note to ask the dyslexia support tutor if it could be provided. Find out how to restock the photocopier with paper or who to ask about this.

Intranet

You need to learn how to use the college's intranet. You will probably have been given a code number to allow you to get on the net and instructions on how to use it. You need to find out how to get an e-mail address, how to send and receive e-mails, and how to access other material on the net, e.g., lecture outlines and dyslexia-friendly software programs.

If you can't understand the written instructions you've been given for using the intranet, then you can, of course, ask another student or a librarian to help you. But you will probably find that when people give instructions about using a computer, they tend to talk very fast and to press a lot of keys without giving you time to see what they are doing.

If this happens, don't just sit there feeling dismayed and bewildered. Point out to your mentor that you are dyslexic and that they need to speak more slowly and perhaps to repeat things. Note down the instructions they give you in a form you can easily understand. If you are fortunate enough to possess a voice recorder, record the instructions and write them down later.

```
┌─────────────────────────────────────────────────────┐
│                    USEFUL TIP!                        │
│                                                       │
│  If you live in or near a town with a big public      │
│  library, it may be worth your while to join this.    │
│  The library may have some of the textbooks or texts  │
│  that you need, and there may be less competition     │
│  for borrowing these than in the college library.     │
│  You will also be able to have the use of a compter   │
│  at the library, either free of charge or for a       │
│  nominal fee.                                         │
└─────────────────────────────────────────────────────┘
```

Loans

Before leaving the library, check with a librarian if, as a dyslexic student, you will be allowed an extended loan period for books.

Stationery

You will need to equip yourself with stationery: ring binders, dividers, folders, plastic file sleeves, A4 pads, etc. When you visit the shop to buy these items, make a note of the shop opening hours. This will save you a wasted journey in future.

Computer equipment

You may wish to buy some computer accessories, e.g., a rewritable CD or a USB key to transfer information between computers. Before purchasing such items, however, check if the college computer system supports them.

There are many software programs which are useful to dyslexic students (see Appendix B for detailed information on these). Some of these may be pre-installed on the college computer system.

Organising and planning activities

In the previous two phases of your introduction to student life, you became familiar with your territory and with the tools and equipment at your disposal. It's now time to move on to the third – and quintessentially human – stage of your evolution: organising and planning activities. In this stage, you need to reflect on the requirements of your course, decide how to organise your time and materials and plan your future work schedule.

Work routines

First and foremost, you need to establish good work routines. Study your timetable and note when you regularly have time free for private study. Try to put at least one hour aside each day to get on with a bit of reading, or making some notes, or whatever else needs doing, even if these things are not immediately urgent. In this way, you build yourself a good base not only of study habits but also of basic knowledge about your subjects, and this will all come in useful when you do suddenly find yourself with a deadline for an essay or an examination to revise for.

Your routines do not have to be rigid; there are many distractions in college life, and there may be days when you just do not feel like working or are unavoidably prevented from doing so. But that doesn't mean that you can't have a clear plan, a well-thought-out routine of study which is always waiting for you when you are in the mood for work. A routine which is not religiously followed is better than no routine at all.

USEFUL TIP!

Pin up copies of your lecture schedule and reading lists somewhere visible in your room.

Keeping track of workload

You need to be able to keep track of your general workload, to be alert to what things are urgent, or will become urgent, and what things can safely be left for an indefinite period. For this, you need a simple 'work pending' system.

Acquire three A4 plastic filing trays, preferably of different colours, and label them respectively:

This week
This month
This term

Any work that needs to be done, any papers that need to be read, any reminders to yourself about things you must do – all these can then be put into the relevant trays. Put each item into a separate file or plastic file sleeve.

At the beginning of each day, go through the 'This week' tray to see what is immediately urgent. If something needs to be done that very day, take it out of the tray and leave it on your desktop. If your desk is a nightmarish chaos of papers and books, don't just throw your urgent work amongst them where it could be lost from sight. Have a particular paperweight to put on the urgent work in order to signal to you that it is sitting there waiting to be done that day.

Then make yourself an **action list** for this urgent work, preferably on a coloured A4 sheet which you can keep with you throughout the day, or on your personal organiser. List the work items in the order you intend to tackle them, and tick off each item clearly when you have done it.

As for the rest of the items in the 'This week' tray, just sort them into some sort of priority. If you have time to tackle some of them that same day, simply add them to your action list.

At the end of the day, check again through the 'This week' tray. If there is something urgent for the following day, put that item out on the desktop under the paperweight where it will get your attention the following morning.

At the end of each week, check through the 'This month' and 'This term' trays to see if the items in them need to be given higher priority. For example, something that has been 'This month' for a week or two may need to move up into the 'This week' tray, and so on.

If you put future reading, e.g., journal articles, into your trays, always mark clearly on the front page of the articles (a) the date by which they must be read, and (b) the date you intend to start reading them.

Planning ahead

Buy yourself, or make, a wallchart which shows you at least three months in advance. Pin this up in your room and be sure to mark on it any deadlines for essays or seminar presentations and, of course, examination dates.

For routine things, like lectures and seminars, you will already have your timetable, but if there are any extra talks, lectures, meetings or seminars coming up, you will need to mark these on your wallchart.

Let's look in detail now at the sort of forward planning you will have to do for:

1   writing an essay;
2   revising for an examination.

Writing an essay

Let's suppose that you are given an essay with a particular deadline. As you start to do the research and preparation for this essay, you will need to ask yourself: are the study periods I have put aside sufficient for me to complete this work before the deadline?

You may well be unable to make a judgement about this initially, but as you proceed with your preparation, you will see how long things are taking you and be able to make some estimate of the total time you will need. Then, if your regular study periods are not enough, you will need to slot in further periods of work, possibly in the evening or at weekends. You may even have to sacrifice treasured social activities to meet your deadlines.

One thing to remember is that, as a dyslexic student, you may be able to request an extension for essay deadlines. Even if you are able to do this, plan your study schedule as if you were going to meet the original deadline – and try to do so; the extra time will then act as a safety net. There is a danger that, if you continually request extensions, you will end up with several essays becoming urgent at the same time and find yourself overwhelmed. (For more detailed information on essay planning, see Chapter 8.)

Revision schedules

One thing which does need good long-term planning is your revision schedule for examinations. You need to work out how much time you want to give to different topics and be clear what you need to do for each topic.

Ask yourself the following questions:

- Do you need to do extra reading, or have you already covered the reading?

- If you've done the reading, have you got notes from it that you can still understand? If you can't understand your notes, you will have to revisit the original books or articles. (See Chapter 6 for advice on note-taking.)
- If you have done the reading and have made clear notes, have you given yourself time to commit the essential points to memory? You may need to do a skeletal plan of model answers for various topics and commit that plan to memory.

So, planning a revision schedule needs an initial period of reflective thought so that you can estimate the time needed for dealing with different topics. If it turns out that the time needed far exceeds the time available to you, then you have to change your revision plan. You may decide to revise fewer topics or to be content with a less detailed knowledge of some of the topics you are covering.

Revision will need to be spread out over at least a term and, probably, through the preceding holiday as well. This is where it's important to have very efficient long-term planning procedures.

Write the names of the revision topics you're going to tackle on index cards – just one topic on each card. Decide which topics you're going to tackle immediately and put the relevant cards in your 'This week' tray. Decide which are the next-most-urgent topics and put the relevant cards in your 'This month' tray. The cards for the topics you're going to tackle last will go in the 'This term' tray. As the exam approaches, the cards should be gradually moving up from 'This term' to 'This month' to 'This week'.

It's also useful to pin up a revision master plan on the wall. On this, list all the topics, both main topics and sub-topics, you will be revising, and tick off each one when you have covered it.

In general, it's a good idea to get into the habit of just glancing through your 'work pending' trays and scrutinising your wall planner and revision chart at odd moments, say, when you're waiting for an egg to boil. The reason for this is that it's helpful always to have in mind a general overview of your work schedule and to know how much of it is urgent or shortly becoming urgent.

Another important element in good organisation is having an efficient filing system and getting into the habit of doing your filing at regular intervals. For more advice on this, see p. 92.

Perhaps you're thinking that all of the above sounds too good to be true; it's great in theory, but in practice you'll never manage all that. Well, maybe you won't. But, as I said at the beginning, you don't have to set impossible standards for yourself. You may not be a super-student when it comes to organising your work schedules and planning ahead, but anything at all you can do in this direction will be of benefit.

Reducing stress and anxiety

Being well-organised will be helpful not just to your studies but also to your own emotional well-being. One of the main disadvantages of always feeling in a muddle is that you go around in a state of constant worry and anxiety. When deadlines suddenly loom, you're ill-prepared for them, so then you tend to overwork and become fatigued, often so fatigued that you actually can't sleep. This sets up a vicious circle of inefficiency, anxiety and fatigue and the result can be – as Clare reported in Chapter 1 – a state of sheer desperation. So, do as much as you can to keep yourself organised. Reflect, plan, prepare.

Also, when you plan work schedules, don't just plan work: plan rest breaks or longer rest periods too. You will work more efficiently if you take regular breaks rather than slogging on and on, getting more tired. Clare devised a particular work routine which allowed her to have rest breaks which got longer the longer she worked. What she did was to work for fifty minutes initially and take a ten-minute break. Then she worked for forty-five minutes and took a fifteen-minute break. Then she worked for forty minutes and took a twenty-minute break. Finally, she worked for half an hour. After that, she took a very long break or did no more work at all that day.

You might like to try a similar routine. You can use the alarm function on your computer to cue the beginning and end of your work and rest periods. Clare, who was something of a Luddite, used a kitchen timer. The important thing is to be very strict about stopping work when the alarm or timer goes off. Finish your sentence, and, if you're worried about forgetting what you're going to say next, make a very quick note and then begin your rest break.

RELAXATION EXERCISE

Sit or lie in a comfortable position. Either close your eyes, or simply lower your gaze so that you feel less aware of your surroundings.

Bring your attention to your breathing. Feel conscious of your in-breath, and the moment's pause which follows it, and then the release of your out-breath.

As you try to concentrate on your breathing, you will no doubt find that a myriad thoughts about other things – and perhaps particularly about the essay you are working on – continually enter your mind. Do not strive to stop these thoughts coming into your mind. Simply notice when a thought is present, and then gently expel this thought with your next out-breath.

If you find that thoughts have somehow 'eluded' your out-breath, and are jostling around in your mind giving rise to further thoughts, don't berate yourself for failure, or feel annoyed with these thoughts. Don't get into a fight with them – just keep quietly breathing them out. Even if you manage only a few seconds breathing out thoughts rather than thinking them, you will have done well, and your mind will have enjoyed some rare moments of relaxation.

Take between 10–20 minutes for this exercise. When you are ready to end the exercise, just sit quietly for two or three minutes letting thoughts come and go at will.

A good tactic to use if you are faced with a large task, such as researching and writing an essay, is, first of all, to get an overall idea of everything you will need to do – what papers or books you will need to read, etc. But then, cease to think of the task as a whole and concentrate on separate bits of it.

For example, if you have a reading list with ten articles on it, in the first stage you need to look at the task as a whole in order to plan how much time you need to set aside for reading ten articles. However, having once roughly planned out a schedule for this, put the phrase 'ten articles', out of your mind and think simply: Article 1.

In this way, when you actually begin working on the task, you are concentrating your efforts on one bit of it. The task as a whole may seem impossible, but one bit is usually manageable. As you read and make notes on each article, tick that article off clearly on your reading list so that you can monitor your progress.

Breaking down large tasks into separate 'chunks' and working on one chunk at a time, reduces stress and helps you concentrate fully on what you're doing.

The main message in this chapter is: time spent getting organised is never time wasted. However pressurised you feel, however anxious to meet a deadline, don't just plunge headlong into things: always take time to plan what you need to do and to prepare any necessary materials. If you follow this rule, you'll find that in the end you will do things more quickly, more efficiently and with less stress. Then, not only will you cope well with your workload but you will also get more satisfaction and enjoyment out of your college life.

Summary

In this chapter you have learnt how to:

- find your way around the college campus;
- deal with library catalogues;
- use college IT systems and other equipment;
- organise your time and materials;
- plan work schedules;
- reduce stress and anxiety.

Chapter 5

Ways of seeing

In Chapter 2, when we looked at the range of difficulties experienced by dyslexic and dyspraxic people, we saw that visual skills were a particular area of weakness. In this chapter I'll be suggesting ways in which you can improve your visual perception.

The term 'perception' covers two things:

1 what your eyes see;
2 how your brain interprets what your eyes see.

To find ways to improve your sight, you need to consult an optician or optometrist. But to help your brain correctly interpret what it sees, you can use a number of self-help strategies, and these are what I shall be discussing in this chapter.

I'm going to consider the topic of visual perception under three headings:

1 Visual tracking;
2 Visuo-spatial skills;
3 Visual stress.

Visual tracking

Visual tracking means keeping track of where you are on a page when you are reading a text. You need to track individual letters in a word, individual words in a sentence and individual sentences in paragraph. You need to know which line you are on and be able to move smoothly from one line to the next.

In this section I'm going to suggest some strategies for reading words, numbers and signs accurately, for keeping your place in a text, and for analysing visual displays of information.

Reading words

Various things can go wrong when you are reading words:

- You could confuse reversible letters, e.g., b d, m w, p g.
- You could see letters in the wrong order, so you might confuse 'was' and 'saw'.
- You could confuse words that look similar, e.g., 'where' and 'were'.
- You could mis-sequence sounds in long words and so read 'conservation' as 'conversation'.
- You could fail altogether to track the letters in a very long word, e.g., 'interdenominational'.

I explained above that perception is a cooperation between eye and brain. Very often, if your eye is struggling to recognise a word, your brain will come to its aid by making an intelligent suggestion based on the context of the word.

For example, in reading the sentence:

I saw that he was making a mistake.

you are unlikely to confuse 'saw' with 'was' and read a nonsensical sentence:

I was that he saw making a mistake.

However, context would not help you accurately read 'conservation' in the following sentence:

He is very keen on conservation.

Because this sentence could make equal sense if you read:

He is very keen on conversation.

So, when you are reading a word, in particular a long word, you need to have efficient strategies for tracking the letters in that word. And here your brain can again come to the aid of your eye. When your eye looks at a word, it sees a lot of – possibly muddling – letter shapes, but when your brain looks at a word, it sees a structure and a meaning. So, to read words efficiently, you need to do some brainwork: you need to understand the structure of words, to see how they are built up from a series of component parts and to be aware that these parts often have a meaning.

To put this another way, you need to get into the habit of seeing words not as a long string of letters, but as a small group of separate building blocks or syllables. For example,

$$conservation = con\ ser\ va\ tion$$
$$conversation = con\ ver\ sa\ tion$$

SPLITTING WORDS INTO SYLLABLES

If you find it difficult to work out just where one syllable in a word ends and another begins, try singing the word to yourself to a well-known tune.

Take the word 'interdenominational'.

This has eight syllables. Can you identify them? If not, sing the word to the tune of 'Auld Lang Syne'.

Should auld ac-quaint-ance be for-got

in   ter de   nom in   a tion al

Once you start splitting up words into their component syllables, you will become aware that the same syllables occur again and again at the beginnings and ends of words. Syllables which are tacked onto the beginnings of words are called 'prefixes', and syllables at the ends of words are called 'suffixes'. Together these two groups are referred to as 'affixes'. Look on pages 65–6 for a list of common affixes.

Having looked at the list, you will see that affixes often have meanings; they operate, in fact, like little words which crop up again and again as parts of longer words. So if you make yourself familiar with these affixes and their meanings, you'll be in a strong position to read long words.

AFFIX PRACTICE

Keeping an eye on pages 65–6, try spotting the affixes in these words:

expression

representing

submariner

contortionist

insightful

uncomfortable

interrelated

incomprehensible

Answers on page 66.

At odd moments – doing things at odd moments is a good habit – practise splitting up words into their syllables and recognising the affixes. Take a relatively short article in a quality newspaper, pick out the long words and try to work out their structure. You will soon find more affixes to add to the list given at the end of this chapter.

From all of the above, you will see that the more you get your brain involved in recognising words, the less work your eyes have to do when you are reading. And, as a bonus, a good understanding of word structure will also help your spelling.

Reading numbers and signs

If your visual tracking is poor, you will be prone to error in reading, copying or writing numbers. In fact, you may find that you are much *more* inaccurate with numbers than with words. And the reason is not hard to find. We saw above that when you are reading words, your eyes are constantly helped by information provided by the brain about context and word structure. But when you are reading numbers, the brain is virtually helpless: it can't use context to make intelligent guesses about the numbers you see, nor can it look for any particular structure in the numbers. So your eyes have to manage on their own.

However, there are some mechanical measures you can take to help the eye. When dealing with a long number, break it down into small chunks by covering parts of the number up. Then read the number, one chunk at a time. A good general rule is to use chunks of two or three digits. So the number:

396069235825

could be read as:

39 60 69 23 58 25

or:

396 069 235 825

If you are copying the number, write down each set of two or three digits, and check it carefully *once only* before moving on to the next set.

Try to avoid *continually* checking and rechecking your work, as this is likely to result in confusion.

In some cases, it may be useful to break the number up in a different way. There may be some sets of component numbers which are particularly easy to remember, perhaps because they make up a date or form an easily recognisable pattern:

63 1902 874
62 88 942 55

Be particularly careful with numbers which contain a string of zeroes:

93000029

With these, it is useful to cover up part of the number with a piece of paper so that you only deal with two zeroes at a time:

9300

and then

0029

Also, take particular care when you have two similar numbers close together. This can often happen with telephone and fax numbers:

tel. 030 7271 2468
fax 030 7271 2487

Cover one of these up while you read or copy the other. When you're in a hurry, it's easy not to bother with something like this. However, for a dyslexic person, there is always a trade-off between speed and accuracy – if you don't find the time to take due care, you could easily finish up making a mistake.

If you own the book you're reading, you could also highlight various sections of a number in colour. If you're working on a computer, you have many more options available to you: you can separate the number into sections or highlight sections with italics or bold print or with different font type or size. Experiment freely to find out what works best for you.

If you are studying a science subject, you may have difficulty in reading equations or chemical formulae. You can deal with these in the same way as you would an ordinary number. Tackle each segment of the equation or formula separately, highlighting or covering up sections of it.

Signs can also be a problem. Get into the habit of looking at them twice. It may also help to speak the sign out loud, or under your breath if you're in the library.

In general, try to work with numbers in a calm and systematic way. Check what you've done once and move on.

Keeping your place on the page

If you have difficulty keeping your place on a printed page or on the computer screen, there are a number of things you can do to keep your eye 'on track'. You could:

- use your finger to keep your place;
- place a standard ruler below the line you're reading;
- use an eye-level coloured ruler (see p. 209);
- use a reading window – this can be simply two pieces of paper or card placed above and below a section of text;
- use a screen-reading ruler.

Analysing visual displays of information

Visual displays of information include such things as graphs, tables of figures, bar charts, pie charts, diagrams and maps. Even if your preferred learning style is to 'visualise' information, you may still find that your eye gets confused when presented with detailed abstract visual data of this sort.

In order to make things easier for your eye, use the same sort of strategies I suggested above for reading numbers. For example, use colour to distinguish lines on a graph, or bars on a chart, or slices of a pie chart or to highlight sections of diagrams or maps.

Also, it's very important to get into the habit of calmly and slowly reading the written information on graphs, etc. This is often in small print and may include easily confused abbreviations, such as 'cm' for centimetre and 'mm' for millimetre. Or it may have fiddly little signs, e.g., '×100' indicating that you need to multiply the figures on the graph by 100 to get the true figure.

When you've carefully and methodically scanned the visual display and have read the accompanying written information, pause and think about what it all means. For here is another opportunity for your brain to come to the aid of your eyes. The more you understand the information before you, the better you will see it.

On the graph in Figure 5.1, for example, what does the data presented actually tell you about the popularity of different subjects studied at college? Does this information surprise you? Do you have any idea why some subjects are so much more popular than others?

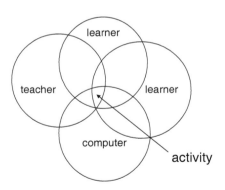

Figure 5.1 The number of students graduating in psychology, medicine, theology and law, 2000–4.

If you are dealing with tables of figures, draw an extra thick line below each third row of figures so that you're always working in segments of three. Any given number will then be at the beginning, in the middle, or at the end of a segment and, therefore, more easily distinguishable. You can help your eye further by colour-coding the different segments.

A simple example of this is the multiplication square below:

	1	2	3	4	5	6	7	8	9	10	11	12
1	1	2	3	4	5	6	7	8	9	10	11	12
2	2	4	6	8	10	12	14	16	18	20	22	24
3	3	6	9	12	15	18	21	24	27	30	33	36
4	4	8	12	16	20	24	28	32	36	40	44	48
5	5	10	15	20	25	30	35	40	45	50	55	60
6	6	12	18	24	30	36	42	48	54	60	66	72
7	7	14	21	28	35	42	49	56	63	70	77	84
8	8	16	24	32	40	48	56	64	72	80	88	96
9	9	18	27	36	45	54	63	72	81	90	99	108
10	10	20	30	40	50	60	70	80	90	100	110	120
11	11	22	33	44	55	66	77	88	99	110	121	132
12	12	24	36	48	60	72	84	96	108	120	132	144

Visuo-spatial skills

Visuo-spatial skill is the ability to see the relation of objects (including yourself) to each other in space. For example, you use these skills when you do a jigsaw, catch a ball, or cross a busy road.

Advice on dealing with visuo-spatial difficulties in everyday life will be given in Chapter 9 (pages 129–32). In this chapter I shall focus on two curriculum subjects in which you have to visualise spatial relationships in the abstract: mathematics and statistics.

Dealing with mathematics and statistics

It might seem that visuo-spatial skills would only be useful in certain aspects of mathematics – geometry, for instance, where one has to work with shapes. In fact, however, the whole of mathematics is basically a spatial subject, and a large part of our mathematical thinking takes place in a part of the brain which specialises in recognising spatial relationships.

To understand this better, think back to how you first learnt arithmetic when you were a small child. I don't imagine that you initially learnt how to add up and subtract in a theoretical way. More probably, someone laid out some buttons or other objects on a table in front of you so that you could *see* the effect of adding and subtracting with your own eyes. When you learnt about multiplying and dividing, probably someone drew you a shape and demonstrated dividing it up or adding further shapes.

Later on, you became able to do these arithmetical operations, and other forms of mathematical calculation, without a visual aid. But, at heart, mathematics remains a spatial subject. It deals with spatial relations: the *measurement* of magnitude, length, volume, etc. Consequently, people with poor visuo-spatial skills (and this includes the majority of dyspraxic people) often have difficulty in grasping the basic concepts of mathematics.

If you are mathematically challenged, I can only suggest that you do not attempt a degree in theoretical physics. However, even if you avoid studying the pure sciences, you may not wholly escape mathematics: it may still ambush you in the guise of statistics in a 'soft science' subject like psychology or economics.

As regards statistics, you could have two levels of ambition. The higher level is to thoroughly understand the mathematical underpinnings of the subject and to be able to wax eloquent on topics such as 'bell curves' and 'variance'. The lower, more pragmatic level, is to learn how to use statistics in practice. At this level you need to:

- know how to choose an appropriate statistical test for a particular experiment or study;
- exercise care in carrying out the relevant calculations (if you are not relying on a computer to do them);

- know how to interpret the results of the test you have used.

So, if you are mystified by the theoretical aspects of statistics, at least become proficient in the practical aspects of the subject.

Visual stress

The term 'visual stress' refers to a difficulty in looking at lines of print or patterns. People who suffer from this syndrome report that print seems to 'jump about', lines appear blurred, and repetitive patterns shift around. They also find that reading in a bright light, especially fluorescent light, is stressful, and that white paper seems to 'glare'.

There are a number of ways of reducing visual stress. You can:

- use coloured paper when you are writing;
- photocopy texts onto coloured paper;
- use coloured overlays when reading;
- use an eye-level coloured reading ruler;
- use a relaxing colour on the computer screen.

For information on where to buy overlays and coloured rulers, see pp. 208–9.

If visual stress causes you a great amount of discomfort, then it is advisable to have a professional assessment by an optometrist *who specialises in colorimetry*. The optometrist will determine which colour or colours suit you best, both for reading text on paper and for reading on the computer screen. He or she may also prescribe tinted lenses. (See page 209 for information on how to find an optometrist.)

Alternative terms for visual stress are: Meares–Irlen Syndrome, pattern glare and scotopic sensitivity. You will find a visual-stress checklist in Appendix A.

COMMON PREFIXES

Prefix	Meaning	Example
ad-	to, towards	advance
con-, com-	together	companion
contra-	against	contradict
de-	down	descend
dis-	not	disbelieve
ex-	out	exterior
in-, im-	in, into	interior, implode
inter-	among	international
mis-	wrongly	mispronounce
mono-	single	monopoly
per-	through	pervade
poly-	many	polysyllabic
post-	after	post-war
pre-	before	pre-war
re-	again	review
sub-	below	submarine
syn-, sym-	together, harmonious	synchronise, symphony
un-	not	unhappy

continued on next page

COMMON SUFFIXES

-able, -ible	capable of, fit for	eatable, edible
-er, -or	doer of an action	painter, director
-ed	shows past time	called, shouted
-ing	shows present time	I am reading
-ess	shows feminine	lioness
-ful	full of	fearful
-ion, -sion, -tion	(1) state of	depression, confusion, elation
	(2) event	explosion, election
-ist	practitioner	chemist
-ity	quality of	tranquillity
-less	without	fearless
-logy	study of	geology
-ness	state of	happiness

Figure 5.2 List of common prefixes and suffixes (affixes).

Answers to affix exercise on p. 55

Affixes are shown in italics:

ex press *ion*
re pre sent *ing*
sub marin *er*
con tort *ion ist*
in sight *ful*
un com fort *able*
inter re lat *ed*
in com pre hens *ible*

Summary

In this chapter you learnt how to:

- read words and numbers accurately;
- keep your place on the page;
- deal with visual representations of data;
- manage statistics;
- get assessment and treatment for visual stress.

Reading and note-taking

Do you often find that, when reading a book or a journal article, you get to the end of it and then realise that you can't remember a single thing about what you've read? If so, don't be too downhearted – you are not alone. Many people have this experience, especially when reading non-fiction; dyslexic readers simply experience this problem in a particularly acute form.

So, how can you help yourself to read more efficiently? In the last chapter, I gave advice on strategies you can use to improve the *accuracy* of your reading; in this chapter, I'll suggest ways in which you can improve your *comprehension*.

Let's start by analysing how you go about reading at the moment. When faced with, say, a long chapter in a book, do you:

- put off reading it indefinitely?
- vaguely skim through it?
- start reading it in a very concentrated way?
- read it through again and again hoping that something 'sticks'?

- dot about in the text hoping to find something easy to understand?

When it comes to reading for comprehension, different people find different strategies helpful, and the most important thing is to find a strategy that helps you. I am going to suggest, however, that none of the strategies listed above is likely to be of much help to a dyslexic reader. In order to understand a text as you read through it and to retain some memory of the main points, it is probably best if you get into the habit of taking notes as you read.

Note-taking is one of the most crucial skills a student needs to learn. It is essential not just for taking notes from books but also for following lectures and planning essays. In this chapter, I shall concentrate on taking notes from books. I shall give three different formats for note-taking and leave you to decide which is best suited to you. You may, in fact, like to use a combination of all three.

Whatever method of note-taking you choose, there are some general points to be made about how to approach this task, and so I will begin with these.

Reconnoitre the ground

A good way of tackling a written text is to think of it as an unknown piece of territory which you need to reconnoitre before you begin a detailed exploration. If you followed the suggestions given at the beginning of Chapter 4 (pp. 31–33), you will already have some experience of physically reconnoitring territory, i.e., your college campus. Now you can do the same thing metaphorically with a text. If possible, get a photocopy of the text you are studying so that you can make notes or highlight words on it.

Distinguish between structure and content

When analysing a text, you need to distinguish between two important components: the *structure* of the text and the *content* of the text. The structure is like an overall map of the text and will be the target of your initial reconnaissance. The content gives detailed information about places on the map and will be the target of your later, more detailed, exploration.

IMPORTANT!

You need to keep your notes on structure separate from your notes on content. Ideally, you should have two A4 pads in different colours, one for structure notes, one for content notes.

Mapping the structure

To map the structure of a text, you need to look for landmarks which will mark out the main sections of the text, for example, sub-headings within a chapter. Some places to look for landmarks are:

- **The Contents page at the beginning of the book.**
  In some books the Contents shows the main topics covered in each chapter. For example, the chapter you are reading now could be shown like this:
  Chapter 6. Reading and note-taking
  Note taking strategies. Mapping structure. Exploring content. Identifying keywords. Linear notes. Visual notes. Tree diagrams. Using notes to plan essays. Abbreviations.
  So, just by looking at the Contents page, you can immediately see the structure of an individual chapter.
- **The beginning of each chapter.**
  In scientific books or papers, there is often an abstract (summary) at the beginning of the chapter which tells you in advance what topics the chapter will cover.
- **The end of the chapter.**
  In many books there is a summary at the end of each chapter, or a final paragraph that sums up the information given in the chapter. (In this book there are end-of-chapter summaries.)

If you are unlucky, and you don't find any of the above landmarks, then you need to work out the structure of the chapter yourself.

Do this by looking for the sub-headings in the chapter and making a note of these on your structure notepad. For example, your structure notes for Chapter 4 of this book would look like this:

Exploring territory
Using tools
  Library catalogue
  Photocopiers
  Intranet
  Loans
  Stationery
  Computer equipment
Organising and planning activities
  Work routines
  Keeping track of workload
  Planning ahead
    Essays
    Revision
  Reducing stress and anxiety.

If you are really unlucky and find yourself reading a chapter where there are no sub-headings, then you have a more challenging task. You have to set out on your reconnaissance exercise without any clear idea of where you might be heading. You just have to hope that on your route you will find some signposts to guide you.

Signposts in this context means *indications* given by the writer about what topics he or she intends to cover in a text. A good place to look for signposts is in the first paragraph of the chapter. The writer may tell you straight away where he or she intends to go in the chapter, in other words what the structure of the chapter will be. *One of the key skills in note-taking is to be able to identify signposts*, and, as you journey through the chapter, *recognise when you have reached the location to which these signposts point.*

Here is an example to make this clear:

Suppose that you are studying psychology, and you are reading a chapter about different types of therapy. The first paragraph might say something like:

> In this chapter, I'm going to discuss various approaches to therapy and to evaluate their effectiveness. I shall deal with three types of therapy: behaviour, cognitive and psycho-dynamic.

There are four signposts in this paragraph. Three of the signposts point to descriptions of different types of therapy (behaviour, cognitive and psycho-dynamic). The fourth signpost points to a discussion on the effectiveness of these therapies.

Highlight each of the four signposts and also note them down on your structure notepad. (If you're working from a library book, miss out the highlighting stage.) You now have an overall map of the chapter.

STRUCTURE NOTES

Three types of therapy: behaviour
                                 cognitive
                                 psycho-dynamic

Effectiveness

Next, look through the chapter, *not trying to understand the text in detail* but trying to spot when the four topics you have highlighted first appear in the text. To do this, you will probably only need to look at the first couple of lines in each paragraph. What you will be looking for is introductory phrases like:

Behaviour therapy is based on a reward and punishment principle . . .

A different approach is represented by cognitive therapy . . .

Finally, psycho-dynamic therapy . . .

An advantage of this approach . . .

Highlight the first appearance (and further appearances if useful) of each topic.

When you have found the phrases you are looking for, note the relevant page number in your structure notes. It's useful to put the paragraph number too. So, page 1, paragraph 2 would be simply 1, 2.

If you are able to spot where each of the main topics is discussed in the text, you will have mapped out the main features of the ground that you will have to cover in the chapter.

You can now turn to a more in-depth exploration of the content of the chapter.

Exploring content

You may recall the suggestion I made above that you provide yourself with two A4 pads in different colours, one for structure notes, the other for content notes. You need to have the second A4 pad, your content notepad, ready now. But please note that, as you immerse yourself in the detailed content of the chapter, it's important to keep your structure notes clearly visible on your desk. Then, if you feel you're getting lost in detail, you can easily get your bearings again by glancing at the structure notes.

Take one section of the chapter at a time. If the sections are particularly long, take half a section at a time. As you begin to concentrate on the content in detail, you can choose between different methods. Some people like to read through a whole paragraph before they start taking notes. Other people, however, find this a waste of time, because they take in nothing of what they read.

You might find it helpful to begin your note-taking as soon as you start reading a paragraph. This has the advantage that, if you take notes on the first paragraph – and so have concentrated on that paragraph and understood what it says – this understanding will make it easier for you to understand the second paragraph, and so on. So it might be best to just plunge straight in with your note-taking.

In taking detailed notes on the text, you will continue to be on the alert for signposts. Look for phrases such as:

- 'There are three main reasons why', (and then look for these three reasons in the next part of the text);
- 'There are several objections to this' (and then look for these objections in the next part of the text);
- 'There are advantages and disadvantages in this method' (and then look for both advantages and disadvantages in the next part of the text).

If you have identified the signposts but have not found the location that they point to, you must have missed something (unless the writer has made a complete mess of the chapter). So go back and make sure you find the text to which the signposts have pointed.

All this has been a bit theoretical, so I'm going to present a short piece of text below and demonstrate how I myself would take detailed notes on its *content*. (Of course, in real life, the texts you have to deal with are much longer, but this short piece will serve our purposes in this chapter.)

I have already made the structure notes for this passage and will repeat them below for easy reference. Then I can have the text structure always in mind as I study the passage for detailed content.

STRUCTURE NOTES

Three types of therapy: behaviour
                       cognitive
                       psycho-dynamic
Effectiveness

My detailed note-taking for content will be in two stages:

1 highlighting keywords;
2 making written notes.

Again, if you are working from a library book, you will have to move straight to Stage 2.

Note: you will find it easier to follow the rest of this chapter if you can take a photocopy of the passage given below.

Highlighting keywords

Taking the passage one paragraph at a time and always keeping in mind the topics in my structure map, I shall underline words which will give me the 'key' to the content of each paragraph.

In this chapter, I'm going to discuss various <u>approaches to therapy</u> and to evaluate their <u>effectiveness</u>. I shall deal with <u>three types</u> of therapy: <u>behaviour</u>, <u>cognitive</u> and <u>psychodynamic</u>.

Behaviour therapy is based on a <u>reward and punishment</u> principle. For <u>example</u>, one way of dealing with a <u>child</u> who is subject to <u>temper tantrums</u> is to promise the child a reward if he or she manages to control their behaviour.

continued on next page

This could be an ice cream or a trip to the zoo, or it could simply be giving praise to the child. Punishment could be making the child forgo a promised treat.

Advantages of behaviour therapy are that it can have quick results and also that the results are usually easily measurable. It would have limitations in dealing with more complex conditions, such as depression.

A different approach is represented by cognitive therapy. This aims to change the pattern of a person's conscious thoughts. For example, a person may tend to feel that, whenever anything goes wrong, they must be somehow to blame. The cognitive therapist will encourage the client to review their habitual thinking patterns and make a conscious effort to change them.

An advantage of this approach is that it gives the client some active control over what's happening; it can produce relatively quick results; and can often be obtained without charge on the NHS. On the other hand, it may not be effective against deep-seated emotional patterns, particularly unconscious resistance to change.

Finally, psycho-dynamic therapy is an open-ended intervention which aims at bringing into consciousness the client's unconscious thoughts and feelings, e.g., feelings for parents. This is done by techniques such as dream analysis and observing the way in which the client reacts to the analyst.

This technique may be more successful than the other two therapies in dealing with unconscious resistances to change, but it does not promise a cure. However, many clients report that an analytic approach has helped them make radical and beneficial changes to their life and has given them a better understanding generally of human behaviour and motivations. On the negative side, it can foster a dependence on the therapist, and there is no objective measure of its effectiveness.

You will notice that, in choosing my keywords, I concentrated on the main points in each paragraph, and didn't get lost in detail.

I suggest you practise this keyword technique on a few passages from your textbooks. You need to develop the art of choosing just enough keywords to quickly give you the main content of the passage – not only at the moment when you are reading it through but also at the later stage when you use the keywords to make your own notes on the passage.

I'll deal with this second, note-taking stage in the next section.

USEFUL TIP!

Use a software program such as textHELP
to read e-mails, web pages or scanned documents
out loud to you.
See p. 196 for more details.

Making written notes

I'm going to suggest three methods of taking notes. (Did you notice that this is a signpost?) I suggest you try out all three and see which suits you best. I'm calling the three methods:

1   The linear method
2   The balloon method
3   The tree method.

In all three methods, your keywords are the basis for your notes.

The linear method

With this method you simply list the main points in the passage. So, if I used this method for the above passage on therapy, my notes would look something like this:

APPROACHES TO THERAPY
1   Behaviour th.
    Reward and punishment (e.g., temper tantrums)
    ✓ Quick, measurable results
    ✗ Complex probs, e.g., depression

2   Cognitive th.
    Change conscious thoughts (e.g., stop blaming yourself)
    ✓ Active, quick, free
    ✗ Doesn't go deep

3   Psycho-dynamic th.
    Make unconscious feelings conscious (e.g., towards parents)
    ✓ Gives in-depth understanding, promotes change
    ✗ May not cure, dependency on therapist, results not measurable

You will see that I kept my notes short by using abbreviations:

- I used ✓ to stand for the phrase: *the advantages of this are* . . .
- I used ✗ to stand for the phrase *the disadvantages of this are* . . .
- I also abbreviated words: 'th.' for 'therapy', 'probs' for 'problems'.

You will find more suggestions for abbreviations on pages 86–7.

Balloon method

If I had used a balloon method for my notes, they might look something like Figure 6.1 on the following page.

As you will see, this separates out the different sections of the passage more clearly by physically separating them on the page. You can colour-code the different sections of the diagram. If you use this type of note-taking, it's important to number, or give letters to, the different groups of ideas to indicate their original order.

The tree method

A third way to take notes – one which may need a little practice before you become efficient with it – is what I call the tree diagram (as it resembles a family tree). This has the advantage that it clearly shows both the structure and the content of the chapter at the

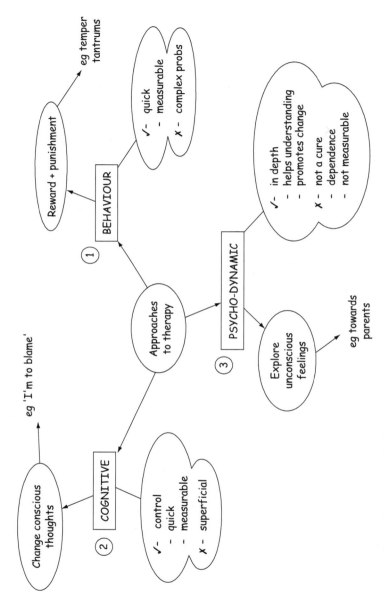

Figure 6.1 The balloon method of taking notes.

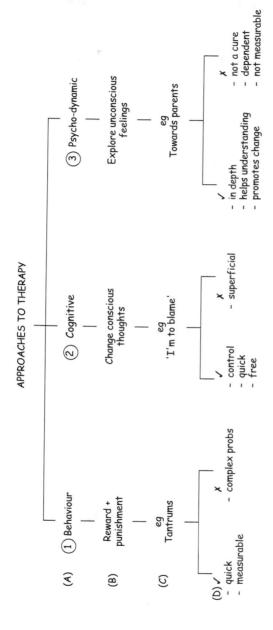

Figure 6.2 The tree method of taking notes.

same time. My tree notes on the above passage could look like Figure 6.2 on page 83.

As you will see, in this method of note-taking, I am showing the structure of the passage visually through the overall structure of the diagram, while the content appears in a series of lists. The various groups of ideas are presented in the same order as they appear in the passage.

Ranged along the top row (A) of the diagram are the names of the three types of therapy. Below these, on the second row (B), is a brief explanation of how each works. After this, on the third row (C), there is a practical example of each. Then, on the fourth row (D), the vertical lines each sprout two branches, one showing the advantages of the therapy, the other the disadvantages.

Seeing the structure and content of a passage presented together in this way will help you not only to understand the passage but also to remember at least something of its content.

This way of taking notes can also be very helpful when you want to use these notes for planning an essay. According to the slant of the essay question, you can easily pick out the relevant bits of the diagram. For example:

If you had an essay on '*Describe the methods of behaviour therapy and appraise its effectiveness*', then you simply need to read off your notes vertically down the left-hand leg of the diagram.

If the essay topic is '*Compare and contrast the methods used by behaviour, cognitive and psycho-dynamic*

therapists',   then   you   can   read   off   your   notes
horizontally along Lines B and C.

If the essay topic is '*What are the respective advantages and disadvantages of behaviour, cognitive and psycho-dynamic therapy?*', then you can read off your notes along Line D.

In the tree diagram above, there were a manageable number of headings: behavioural, cognitive and psycho-dynamic. But if you have many more headings to note down, say seven or eight, don't scrunch them all up on one page; simply extend your family tree onto a second page, or more if necessary, and tape the pages together so that you have a continuous diagram in front of you.

Making notes on a written text, in one or other of the above ways, will help not just your understanding of what you have read but also your recall of it. The fact that you have had to concentrate hard on the content of the text and to reproduce it in summary form will strengthen the memory trace of this material in your brain, making it more likely that you will remember it at a later date.

Abbreviations

One way to speed up note-taking is to use abbreviations. There are two kinds of abbreviations: (a) for words and (b) for phrases.

Words

It is important to have a basic set of abbreviations for words that come up frequently.

A few examples of common words and suggested abbreviations are:

rep = represent
conc = conclusion
argu = argument
hyp = hypothesis
lit = literature
meas = measure(ment)
approx = approximately

You can also use text-messaging abbreviations.

You need gradually to build up a bank of abbreviations relevant to your subject. It's no good using masses of abbreviations which you are later unable to interpret. So begin with just a few, and when you can reliably recognise these, add more to your list.

Phrases

You can abbreviate whole phrases, using either letters or signs. For example:

acc   according to

✓   • The advantages of this are . . .
     • An argument in favour of this is . . .
     • Evidence which supports this view is . . .

✗   • The disadvantages of this are . . .
    • An argument against this is . . .
    • Evidence which goes against this view is . . .
→   • This resulted in . . .
    • The consequence of this was . . .

←   • This resulted from . . .
    • This was the consequence of . . .

Give your imagination full rein in thinking up signs or images which will be helpful to your note-taking. Here are a couple more to inspire you:

Henry 8 ☺ wife 6.
Henry VIII was very contented with his sixth wife.

Pope ☹ Henry 8.
The Pope was very discontented with Henry VIII.

The note-taking skills you have learnt in this chapter are crucial to many aspects of your studies. You will need the same skills again when you take notes in lectures or make your own notes for essays – two topics which I shall be discussing respectively in Chapters 7 and 8. So, may I suggest that, before moving on to these chapters, you reread this chapter a couple of times and practise the various note-taking methods described in it. It's very important that you adopt and develop a method with which you yourself feel comfortable and secure.

Summary

In this chapter, you have learnt how to:

- take notes from books;
- distinguish between the structure and content of a text;
- look for landmarks or signposts which will show you the structure;
- use keywords to understand the content;
- use three note-taking formats: linear, balloon and family tree;
- use abbreviations.

Chapter 7

Ways of remembering

Memory is important in all aspects of study and, indeed, of daily life. In Chapter 4 we looked at ways of organising yourself so that you could reliably remember your lecture timetable and study schedule. In this chapter, I shall suggest memory strategies for:

1 remembering non-routine activities;
2 remembering where you have put things;
3 following instructions and explanations;
4 remembering what you have read;
5 note-taking in lectures;
6 giving presentations in seminars.

Remembering non-routine activities

On any given day, a number of thoughts may occur to you about things that need to be done. You might decide you need to arrange an appointment with your tutor, or find a particular book in the library, or give your parents a ring.

Again, other people might give you information that you want to remember: the name of a useful journal, the time of a lecture, the venue for a party.

It's not a good idea to keep all these odd thoughts, intentions and plans busily buzzing around in your brain. Not only do they take up space and energy but they are also a source of anxiety: you will constantly be thinking, will I remember that later? Or, more likely, what was it I meant to do?

So, make things easier for yourself by getting memory back-up in the form of a small *pocket notebook* (or electronic organiser), which you carry around with you at all times. Into the notebook you can put: reminders about things you need to do, a note of useful information you've been given, the title of a book your tutor has recommended, an idea you've had for a poem, the time of a train . . .

Keep the items clearly separated, and give any urgent items one or two stars. When an item has been dealt with, cross it off the list clearly. At the end of every day, look through your notebook, and check that the urgent items have been attended to.

Some of the reminders you've written down for yourself may be about things which are not immediately urgent. In such cases, transfer the non-urgent items to your work-pending trays (see p. 41).

To do this efficiently, keep a small notepad in a bright colour, say red, on your desk, and transfer the items from your notebook to the red pad, one item to a page. Then put the pages in the appropriate trays. An example of this might be:

You've just been told that you have a month to write an essay and have jotted down a reminder to yourself in your notebook to get the relevant books/ journal articles out of the library. You know you won't have time to look for these in the current week, but it's important to get them as soon as possible. So, when you get home, transfer this reminder to a sheet of red paper and put the paper in the 'This month' tray. At the end of the week, when you routinely go through your 'This month' tray, you will be able to transfer this particular note to the 'This week' tray, and so will have your reminder waiting for you at the appropriate time.

In this way, your notebook and your work-pending trays act as a sort of tangible memory system. You can physically put certain things at the forefront of your memory, others on the back burner, and you can constantly review what items are becoming urgent. Not only will this make you more efficient, it will relieve you of the nagging worry that you have forgotten something important.

It does take some discipline to follow these memory routines. It's easy just to think to yourself, 'Oh, I'm sure to remember that, I won't bother to note it down.' But do try to get into the habit of automatically backing up your memory in the ways described above. During your time at college you need to have your mind as free as possible to concentrate on *thinking*; you don't want to clutter it up with constant worries about *remembering* things.

Remembering where you have put things

Dyslexic students often report that they are constantly forgetting where they have put things. Their desk and, indeed, their room, is such a chaos of books, files and half-eaten takeaways that they can't put their finger on the things they need at the moment they need them.

The first thing to do here is to get your papers in order by creating something that at least pretends to be a filing tray or cabinet. You could use a tough cardboard box or a large plastic basket. Keep your files corralled in this, not in an untidy heap but just as they would be in a real filing cabinet – upright, so that you can see the names of the files. The files should, of course, be in alphabetical order. Keep an alphabet arc to hand (see p. 36). It helps to have different coloured files for different subjects.

If some of your paper files contain printouts from computer files, ensure that both the paper and computer files are given exactly the same name.

You need to be disciplined about keeping your files in their proper place. *Try to have a tidy-up at the end of each day.* Designate a particular time when you will check your pocket notebook and your action list (see p. 42), look through your work-pending trays and do your filing. Theoretically, you should have nothing on your desk which is not for your immediate attention.

USEFUL TIP

If you regularly lose things such as your keys, mobile phone, USB, or spectacles, give them a designated 'rest area' in your room – for example, a small basket on your desk.

Following instructions and explanations

There will be many occasions when you have to listen to instructions or explanations. Perhaps your tutor will tell you how to carry out an experiment or a research project. Or a lecturer will explain the theoretical underpinnings of some procedure or the meaning of technical terms. Will you remember all of this later?

If you possess a voice recorder, use it in any situation where you are listening to instructions or explanations. If you don't have a recorder, and you feel you haven't understood something important, ask the tutor to explain it to you again.

You don't need to have the embarrassment of holding up a whole seminar while you seek further guidance; you can contact the tutor afterwards, in person, by telephone or by e-mail, to explain your dyslexic difficulties and ask for extra help. For example, you could ask that instructions be given to you in writing.

If your tutor is clueless about dyslexia, photocopy Chapter 11 of this book and give it to him or her. If you don't make the effort, or can't summon up the courage, to ask for help, you could waste hours writing the wrong essay or carrying out the wrong experiment. If you really don't feel able to approach a tutor yourself, ask the dyslexia support coordinator to contact the tutor on your behalf.

Remembering what you have read

In Chapter 6, I explained how taking notes on a written text can aid both your *understanding* and *recall* of the text. I'm now going to look at further ways in which you can improve your *recall* of what you have read. I'm going to present the following memory strategies:

- visualisation;
- association;
- dramatisation;
- cogitation;
- representation;
- discussion;
- relaxation;
- revision.

To illustrate these strategies, I'm going to take as an example of text the passage on pages 77–8 which describes different types of therapy. Please look back to this now and read it through again a couple of times. Then read on:

Visualisation

Try visualising situations in which the three therapy techniques might be used. For the behavioural technique, visualise a child having a temper tantrum and kicking a table. For the cognitive therapy, visualise a friend telling you they have no self-confidence. For the psycho-dynamic therapy, pretend you are a therapist and visualise your client lying on a couch and delving into childhood memories.

Association

To further distinguish these three types of therapy, associate each of the three people above with different rooms in your house. The child could be in the living room. Your friend could be sitting chatting with you in the kitchen. And your client would be in your office or consulting room.

Dramatisation

Imagine what you would be saying or doing in each of the three cases mentioned above. (It doesn't matter that you're not a therapist yourself and that you may not do exactly what a professional would. The point is to think about the situation, put your imagination to work on it, and so fix it in your mind.) How would you quieten the child? Would you use physical restraint? Would you promise a treat or threaten a punishment?

As to your unconfident friend, how could you persuade him or her to question their habitual way of thinking about themselves and to adopt a more assertive attitude?

With your client on the couch, what sort of things might they be telling you? Their childhood experiences? Something nasty in the woodshed?

Cogitation

Cogitation, or in simpler terms, pondering on something, is a good way to fix that something in your memory. So think about the three types of therapy, particularly about the advantages and disadvantages of each. What do you feel about the three approaches?

Representation

Some people find it useful to represent what they need to remember by a picture. So the child kicking the table could be represented by a quick sketch of a table, the unconfident friend by a head with a lot of question marks over it, and the psycho-dynamic therapy by a sketch of a couch.

Discussion

Take every possible opportunity to discuss the three therapy approaches with fellow students or with lecturers. You may like to form, or take part in, a revision group, in which you discuss this and other topics on your syllabus. You could take turns to present a topic – teaching a topic is an excellent way of committing it to memory.

Relaxation

When trying to commit large amounts of information to memory, make sure that you allow yourself periods of rest and relaxation between the periods of concentration needed for memorising.

Revision

Revisit the notes you have made on a topic after a day or two. (To be sure you do this, put them in your 'This week' tray.) Check that you can make sense of them and that you can remember the meaning of all the abbreviations and signs that you have used.

Note-taking in lectures

One area of study in which memory, in particular short-term memory, is crucially important is note-taking in lectures. When you are taking notes from a book, you have time to read and reread passages and to work out the important things to note down. In a lecture, however, you have only one chance to get down the important points.

As far as actual note-taking skills are concerned, if you have worked through the previous chapter carefully, you should be reasonably proficient at this. You will, for example:

- be alert for signposts which tell you the overall structure of the lecture;
- be alert for key words;
- have a system of note-taking which you feel comfortable with;
- have a set of abbreviations and signs which you are confident you can recognise.

It may be that the lecturer has done some of the note-taking work for you by providing an outline of the lecture on the college intranet. In this case, read through the outline carefully before the lecture. Then, during the lecture, add detailed content information as necessary.

If, however, no outline is provided, then you are faced with a complicated task: you have to take in everything the lecturer is saying, try to work out the structure of the lecture as you go along and also make detailed notes on the content.

Let's suppose you are attending a lecture on the history of the English language. The first part of the lecture is given below. BUT PLEASE DON'T READ IT YET!

I would like you to listen to, and take notes on, this passage before you read it. So, if possible, ask a friend to read the passage to you, or, if you have text-to-speech software on your computer, scan in the text and have the computer read it to you.

When you have finished this exercise, read the passage through and look critically at the notes you have made. Did you work out the structure? Did you get some information down on the main topics? Did you make use of abbreviations? If you're not happy with your notes, think carefully about where you went wrong and how you might improve your note-taking in future.

Now here is the passage, followed by my own notes on it:

ROOTS OF ENGLISH

The English language that we speak today has three main roots: Anglo-Saxon, Latin and Greek.

Anglo-Saxon came to these shores around the fourth century AD when invaders or immigrants came over to Britain from northern Europe.

The second root language of English is Latin, the language of the Roman Empire, of which we were briefly a part. Latin was at first the language of the church, but it began to influence spoken English after the Norman conquest in 1066. The Normans spoke French, which is a Latin-based language, and, after 1066, French became the language of the ruling class in England. So, many Latin-based words entered English indirectly through Norman French.

The third root language is Greek, which had its greatest influence on English during the Renaissance period, in the fifteenth and sixteenth centuries, when there was renewed

continued on next page

---

interest in the ancient world. Greek words were brought into use for newly required medical and scientific terms, e.g., 'telescope'.

Anglo-Saxon was an everyday colloquial language and was characterised by short words, often of irregular spelling, for example, 'high'. Latin and Greek were characterised by long regular words which had prefixes and suffixes tacked on to a word stem. Examples of words derived from Latin and Greek respectively are 'comprehensive' and 'sympathetic'.

The main reason for the richness of modern English is that it combines these two different traditions: a colloquial Anglo-Saxon tradition and an educated Latin-Greek tradition. One result of this is that we usually have two ways of expressing an idea, a short Anglo-Saxon way and a lengthier Latin or Greek way. For example, you have a choice between Anglo-Saxon 'get' and Latin 'receive', or between Anglo-Saxon 'book lover' and Greek 'bibliophile'.

My notes

If I were taking notes on this lecture, I would be alert for signposts at the beginning of the lecture which would point me in the direction of the main topics to be covered. And the lecturer obliges me in this. She begins her talk by *specifying the three main roots of English* she will be discussing: Anglo-Saxon, Latin and Greek.

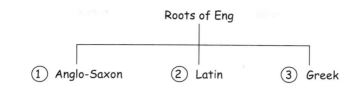

Figure 7.1

My preferred form of note-taking is the tree diagram, and so, at this point, before the lecturer says anything else, I would begin my diagram as above (see Figure 7.1):

As the lecturer continues to speak, I realise that she is explaining *when and how these three languages came into Britain.* She helps me follow her through this section by giving further signposts:

- 'The second root language . . .'
- 'The third root language . . .'

So I can now add this information to my diagram (see Figure 7.2):

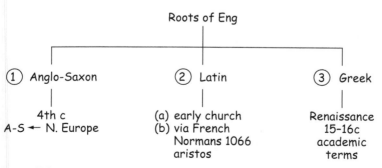

Figure 7.2

After the lecturer has explained how the third language, Greek, came into English, it seems likely that she will move to a new topic – and she does: she begins to describe the *characteristics of the three root languages*. So I can now add this information to my diagram (Figure 7.3).

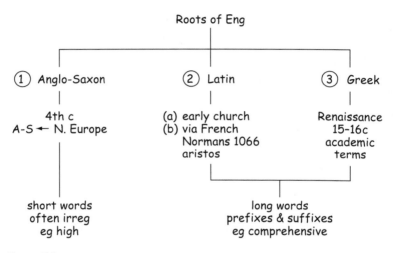

Figure 7.3

Finally, the lecturer makes a point about the *richness* of the English language, and gives a couple of *examples*. So I find a way to show this on my diagram (Figure 7.4).

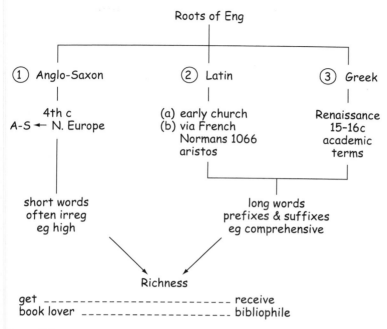

Figure 7.4

When you are listening to a real lecture, you will, of course, have much more information to take down than in this practice exercise. But if you follow the principles outlined above – listening for signposts to the structure of the lecture and trying to mirror this in your notes – you should be able to find your way through even the longest lecture.

You may prefer to take notes using the linear or balloon method (see pp. 80–1) rather than the tree method shown above. If you use the linear method, and you number various points with 1, 2, 3, etc., don't use these same numerals again at a later point in your notes, as this could lead to confusion. Instead use A, B,

C . . . or a, b, c . . . If you run out of letters or numbers, do variations, such as numbers in a circle or with double underlinings.

You may be fortunate enough to have the use of a digital voice recorder to record lectures, and, of course, this is excellent back-up (provided you position the microphone correctly). However, do not get into the habit of just sitting back and letting the recorder do the work. For a start, they sometimes malfunction and may not record all of the lecture. But, more importantly, you need to come away from the lecture with a reasonably good idea of its structure and content. Then, if you have missed bits of the lecture, you can quickly home in on the sections of the recording that you need. What you don't want to do is to sit through the lecture once, and then go home and sit through it all over again on your voice recorder. It doesn't take rocket science to work out that this is doubling your workload.

Giving presentations in seminars

If your tutor asks you to present a topic at a forthcoming seminar, you might well find yourself seized by panic. Most people feel nervous about speaking in public, and, as a dyslexic person, you will have a number of extra anxieties. Will you remember what you want to say? Will you find the words you need? Will you manage to pronounce long words correctly? Will you be able to present your ideas in a clear and logical sequence?

Some people feel so nervous about giving a talk that they write out the whole text of their talk beforehand. But try not to do this: not only is it a waste of time and energy but reading verbatim from a text will make your presentation sound stilted. Rather, write yourself some very clear notes for your talk.

As usual, you need to be clear about both the overall structure of the talk and the detailed content. Make your structure notes on an A4 sheet and keep this in view as you speak. This will help you keep a logical thread in your talk.

As regards the content of your talk, you could note down the points you want to make on a series of index cards, and then all you have to do on the day is to work your way through these.

WARNING!

It is all too easy, especially if you are dyspraxic, to drop your index cards on the floor and, as with Humpty Dumpty, be unable to put them back together again.

So *number* your index cards.
You could also use different coloured cards for different sections of your talk.

If you are worried about not finding the words you want, or mispronouncing long words, I suggest that you act assertively and inform the tutorial group at the beginning of your talk that you are dyslexic and may experience some problems. This will reduce the likelihood of embarrassment, both on your side and on theirs.

It's a good idea to practise giving your talk beforehand to a mirror, using your index cards as cues. If you find at this stage that your notes are not clear, you will have the opportunity to improve them. You will also see how long the talk lasts and whether you need to shorten or lengthen it.

If, after your presentation, people ask you questions which you can't answer, don't get flustered. Just make a note of the questions and say that you will find the answers later and report back.

This is a good example of something which, as a dyslexic student, you need to become very practised at – that is, finding a way to create space and time for yourself in a situation where you are under pressure to make a rapid and impromptu response.

Summary

In this chapter you have learnt how to:

- ensure you remember to do non-routine tasks;
- remember where things are;
- follow instructions and explanations;
- remember what you have read;
- follow and take notes in lectures;
- remember your material when you are giving a talk.

Chapter 8

Academic writing

In this chapter, we'll look at another major study skill: writing in an academic manner. I'll be discussing:

- researching material for an essay;
- writing an essay;
- writing a scientific report;
- writing in examinations;
- writing at the postgraduate level.

Researching material for an essay

Let's suppose that you attend a seminar and are told by your tutor that you have to write an essay on a particular subject by the end of term. The tutor hands you a reading list and suggests some web sites you can look into.

Before you leave the seminar, be quite sure in your own mind that you have fully understood the essay question that has been given to you. If you have uncertainties about it, ask for further clarification from the tutor, either in the seminar or afterwards. As I said earlier in the book, there is absolutely no point spending hours and weeks writing the wrong essay.

Furthermore, if, during your course work, you get into the habit of focusing clearly on the requirements of essay questions, this will stand you in good stead later when you are writing examinations. One of the things that so often goes wrong for dyslexic students in examinations is that they misread or misunderstand questions.

So far so good. But, having understood what you are supposed to be writing about, how do you actually go about doing it? How do you start on your essay project? Do you put it out of your mind for the time being, or do you rush to the library and start frantically reading through the articles on the reading list?

Neither of these things is particularly helpful. The best thing is to scrutinise the list, check which articles on it seem most relevant to your essay topic and make a rough estimate of the time it might take you to read and make notes on these articles.

If it's the first time you've attempted an essay like this, you may have no idea how long it will take you to read the articles, so in that case go and make notes on *one* of the articles and see how you get on with it. This will give you an idea of how many hours approximately you need to set aside for reading and note-taking. If the end of term is six weeks away, it might be useful, for instance, to give yourself a month to do the reading and two weeks to do the writing.

As regards note-taking, I have already given you detailed notes on three note-taking techniques in

Chapter 6 (pp. 80–5). I shall say more about structuring essays later in this chapter.

If you do the reading carefully and make good notes, it should not take you long to write the essay. If you do the reading in a careless way and finish up with a chaotic set of notes, it could take you for ever to write the essay. So focus on each stage of the process as you do it, and do it properly. Don't rush through the reading to get to the writing.

USEFUL TIPS ON DOING RESEARCH FOR AN ESSAY

- Be selective in your note-taking: make sure your notes are relevant to your particular essay.
- Make a careful note of the reference details for the articles or books you consult. Your college will require you to present these in a particular format. For example:

Moody, S. (2007) *Dyslexia: Surviving and Succeeding at College*, London and New York: Routledge.

When you arrive in the library with your reading list, your first task is to find the books and journals you need. If you followed the advice given in Chapter 4 (pages 34–7) about learning to use tools, you will already have had a practice run on this. If you have not had a practice run, don't be surprised if the couple of hours you have allocated to reading is actually spent trying to understand the library system and finding the books.

Don't start by collecting all the books or articles on your list. First, sit down and look carefully through the list. Let's say there are ten journal articles on it. Probably they are given in date order, with the earliest articles first. It might seem logical to start with the earliest articles, but, in fact, it is much more useful to start with the more recent ones. The reason is that the more recent articles will probably include summaries and reviews of the earlier articles, and having these to hand will make reading the earlier articles much easier.

In reading through the articles, you may come across technical terms whose meanings are unclear. Make a note of these terms so that you can look them up in a dictionary or ask your tutor about them later.

USEFUL TIP!

For help with structuring written work, use a software program such as Inspiration. For more information, see p. 198.

Writing an essay

As a practice exercise in this chapter, I am going to notionally write an essay on a general subject on which all my readers may have some opinions: *Describe ways in which tutors can support dyslexic students at college.*

In planning and writing the essay, I shall go through the following stages:

1   Studying the essay title;
2   Brainstorming for ideas;
3   Grouping my ideas;
4   Ordering my ideas;
5   Reminding myself about signposting my ideas to the reader;
6   Writing the introduction;
7   Writing the main text;
8   Writing the conclusion.

Studying the essay title

I need to begin by making sure I have understood *exactly* what I am being asked to write about. I need to study the essay title and underline key words. I note that, in this essay, I am being asked to *describe* something. (In other essays I could be asked to *explain, appraise, review the evidence for*, etc.)

Brainstorming for ideas

Brainstorming means letting my mind rest on the topic in question and noting down any ideas that come to me *on that topic*. I don't need to worry at this stage whether I will eventually use all these ideas or not; I just note them all down.

When I've written down everything I can think of, I look over my ideas critically and check that they are relevant and sensible. I clearly cross out any that are not.

For my essay on things a tutor could do to help dyslexic students, I have decided that the following six ideas are relevant and sensible:

1   Don't ask me to read out loud;
2   Explain how to structure an essay;
3   Help me organise a revision schedule;
4   Star important items on reading lists;
5   Don't be hard on spelling;
6   Advise me on time management.

Of course, if I were writing a real essay, I would have to think of more than these six points. However, for the sake of clarity in this demonstration exercise, I shall confine myself to the above six ideas.

I'm now ready to move on to the next stage:

USEFUL TIP! WRITING AN ESSAY

- Keep referring back to the essay question to make sure you are not wandering off the point.
- Make sure you give evidence for any statements that you make about research findings.

Grouping my ideas

In the previous stage, I just put my ideas down in the form of a list (though I could equally well have written them down randomly anywhere on the page). In this next stage, I'm going to consider whether I can *group* these ideas in some way.

On reflection, I decide I can put the six ideas into three groups:

Reading   Don't ask me to read out loud.
                    Star important items on reading lists.
Organisation   Advise me on time management.
                    Help me organise a revision schedule.
Writing   Don't be hard on spelling.
                    Explain how to structure essays.

As you see, I have continued here to present my ideas in a list. However, at this stage, I could, if I wished, switch to using a balloon or tree diagram. To refresh your memory on these, see pp. 80–85.

Now I'm almost ready to start writing the essay. But there is one last thing to consider: what is the best *order* for the three groups?

Ordering my ideas

I decide I'll begin with the organisation section, as good organisation is a first priority in student life. Then I'll go on to the more specific sections on reading and writing.

So I rearrange my list as follows:

Organisation   Advise me on time management.
                    Help me organise a revision schedule.
Reading   Don't ask me to read out loud.
                    Star important items on reading lists.
Writing   Don't be hard on spelling.
                    Explain how to structure essays.

If you're not working on a computer and can't easily rearrange the groups, just number them 1, 2, 3.

I have now completed all the preliminary planning stages for my essay, so all I have to do now is to sit down and write it.

Reminding myself about signposting my ideas to the reader

While writing my essay, I shall keep my essay plan, my 'map', clearly visible on my desk before me. Thus, at all times, I shall know where I am in the essay. I shall know, metaphorically speaking, what ground I have already covered and where I am heading next.

All well and good – for me. But what about my readers? Will they easily be able to follow me? Will *they* be able to see where I am going in my essay and keep company with me to the end?

If you think back for a moment to the note-taking exercises we did in Chapters 6 and 7, you will recall that, in the passages you studied, the writer/speaker was careful to give signposts to indicate the direction in which she was heading. And she also gave a big hint when she arrived at the location she had signposted.

For example, in the passage on pp. 99–100, the speaker signalled at the beginning of the lecture that she would talk about three languages, and then, later in the lecture, used phrases such as 'the second language . . .', 'the third language . . .' to let her hearers know that she had reached the relevant point in the lecture.

Now that I myself am writing an essay, I need to 'return the compliment' and give clear signposts to my audience.

My first, and biggest, signpost will be in the introduction to the essay.

Writing the introduction

In the introduction, I shall give my readers an overview of my essay, mentioning the main topics *in the order* that I am going to write about them. So the introduction might read as follows:

> *In this essay, I shall consider various ways in which college tutors can offer help and support to dyslexic students. In particular, I shall suggest ways in which tutors can deal sympathetically with three main areas of dyslexic difficulty: organisational skills, reading and written work.*

Short but to the point. Now I can begin the essay proper.

Writing the main text

In writing the main part of the essay, I won't go wrong if I stick doggedly to my essay plan. But I need to continue to give signposts to my readers and to let them know when I have reached the locations to which the signposts point.

So I might start the first paragraph of the essay as follows:

Dyslexic students often have poor organisational skills.

Having got started on the topic of organisation, I might be tempted to plunge enthusiastically into detail on this subject. But that would be a mistake. A glance at my essay plan shows me that I am going to discuss just two aspects of organisational skills: time management and organising a revision schedule.

So I need to signpost these two topics. I could do this by continuing as follows:

They have particular difficulty, for example, with time management and organising a revision schedule.

Then I need to signal to my reader at which point in the essay I start to discuss each of these topics. So I could introduce the two topics with phrases such as:

- *Advice on time management is very helpful to a dyslexic student . . .*
- *A well-thought-out revision schedule is essential . . .*

When I leave the topic of organisation and move to the second topic, reading, I need to the signal this very clearly:

The second topic I am going to consider is reading . . .

Then I shall again signpost the two aspects of the topic I am going to discuss. I shall continue in this way throughout the essay, *always telling my reader where I am going and when I have got there.* In this way, I shall hope to find my reader still close by my side when I reach the end of the essay.

Writing the conclusion

I need to round off my essay with a conclusion. Whereas, in the introduction, I told my reader what topics I intended to cover in the essay, in the conclusion I need to summarise what topics I have covered and to make some general statement about what I have concluded.

So my conclusion could read as follows:

In this essay, I have suggested ways in which tutors could help dyslexic students who have difficulties with organisational skills, reading and written work. There is no doubt that a sympathetic tutor can make all the difference to a dyslexic student's experience at college.

My essay is now finished! I can pour myself a glass of wine and spend the rest of the evening feeling virtuous . . .

> *READ MORE!*
>
> The question of how tutors can help dyslexic students is a very important one. In this chapter, obviously, I have treated it very briefly, as I'm just using it for the purpose of illustrating a good essay-writing technique. However, in Chapter 11, you will find a much fuller guide written especially for tutors.
>
> As you will see, in that chapter I have taken the easy way out and have structured my material not as an essay, which needs signposts, but as a series of sections with sub-headings which act as obvious landmarks for my reader.
>
> If your tutor needs educating about dyslexia, give him or her a photocopy of Chapter 11.

Writing a scientific report

Writing a scientific report is, in many respects, easier than writing an essay. With an essay, you yourself have to decide on the structure of what you write; by contrast, scientific reports usually have standard formats which you can follow. So, the skill in writing these reports is not in working out the structure but in putting the right information in the right sections of the report.

Different sciences may use slightly different report formats, but most reports would include the following sections:

Abstract (summary);
Purpose of study;
Background;
Subjects used in study;

Materials used in study;
Method (or Procedure);
Results;
Discussion.

Let's suppose that you have to write a report on an experimental study you have done. The purpose of your study was to compare the oral reading speed of dyslexic students with that of non-dyslexic students. Your report could read as follows:

Purpose of study

You state your purpose as:

> To determine if dyslexic students are slower at oral reading than their non-dyslexic peers at different levels of text difficulty.

Background

Here you explain why you decided to do this particular study. You refer to previous literature on the subject which suggests that dyslexic students generally do read more slowly than non-dyslexic students but say that you want to explore this topic further and find out if the difference is found for different levels of text difficulty.

Subjects used in study

You report that you tested forty students, twenty of whom had been identified as dyslexic, while the other twenty reported no dyslexic difficulties. You note the ages, sex and areas of study of the students.

Materials used in study

You report that you used three reading passages: an easy passage from a school textbook, a passage of medium difficulty from a student textbook and a very complex passage from a scientific journal.

Method (or Procedure)

Here you describe the conditions in which you administered the tests to all forty students and note that you scored their oral reading speed. You give precise details of your procedure so that another researcher can repeat your experiment, if necessary.

Results

You report that the dyslexic students are slower than their non-dyslexic peers at reading all three texts, and you describe the statistical tests you used to see if the results are significant. Note that you do *not* attempt any discussion of the results in this section.

Discussion

Here you discuss your results and relate these to the results of previous studies. You reflect on whether any problems arose during the experiment which could cast doubt on its validity. Then you draw your overall conclusions and suggest further studies which could be carried out on the same topic.

This is the end of the report, but not quite the end of your work on it. You still need to write an abstract (summary) of the report, which will go at the beginning of your text. The abstract should be short and yet manage to give the reader an overview of the whole report.

Your abstract is as follows:

The purpose of this study was to investigate whether dyslexic students were slower than non-dyslexic students in oral reading of text at different levels of difficulty. Three reading passages of different levels of difficulty were given to a group of forty students, half of whom had been identified as dyslexic. The results, which were statistically significant, showed that the dyslexic students were slower in reading all three passages. The study therefore provides strong evidence that slowness in oral reading at all levels of text difficulty is a good indicator of dyslexia. Suggestions for further studies on this topic are also made.

As you can see, the abstract is really a thumbnail sketch of the whole report. It may not always be easy to keep the abstract short, but do your best: a long abstract is a poor abstract.

USEFUL TIP!

When writing scientific terms be careful not to confuse similar words, e.g.,

lactose   lactase
phenol   phenyl

If such pairs of words crop up regularly in your work, devise a strategy that will help you to distinguish them. For example, you might say the word out loud yourself, emphasising the 'confusable' part of it, as you write or copy it.

Long scientific terms can be broken up into smaller meaningful segments (not necessarily as small as syllables) in the way described on p. 54. For example:

deoxyribonucleic
de oxy ribo nuc leic

Writing in examinations

As regards writing in examinations, you don't have many new tricks to learn. If you have worked through this chapter, you will have all the strategies you need for planning and writing an essay. You will, however, have to take particular care over the following:

- keeping yourself calm;
- reading the questions correctly;
- writing to a strict time limit.

At the beginning of the examination, you may feel nervous and flustered. Your first thought as you look at the examination paper may be that you must somehow have got into the wrong exam: none of the questions seem to make any sense. Even worse, while you are staring in dismay at the paper, everyone around you seems to be busily and confidently writing away.

The way to deal with this is to give yourself five minutes or so to look carefully through the paper without writing anything. If, at first, you feel too panic-stricken to do anything, just sit quietly, take some deep breaths and wait until you feel calmer.

Ignore the fact that the people around you are scribbling away. It obviously suits them to get 'stuck in' straight away. However, if you're dyslexic, this will probably not suit you. You need to do the sort of reconnoitring that you learnt about in connection with note-taking in Chapter 6 (pp. 69–70).

So read carefully through the questions. Read each question twice and highlight keywords in it. Decide which questions you are going to answer and in which order. Note how much time you will have to answer each question.

USEFUL TIP!

As a dyslexic student, you will be entitled to extra time and rest breaks during an examination.

If you are completely overcome by panic in an examination and find yourself unable to write anything, speak to the invigilator and explain that you feel unwell. Ask if it is possible to leave the examination room for an accompanied rest break.

During the break, sit quietly and do deep-breathing exercises. Don't feel you need to justify your situation to the person who accompanies you during the break – just explain that you're trying to deal with a panic attack. For more advice on coping with a panic attack, see pp. 131 and 156–8.

When you return to the examination room, try to get started on answering an examination question by brainstorming for ideas and noting down whatever comes into your head.

Now focus on the first question you are going to tackle. Read the question through once more and ask yourself: do I know *exactly* what this question is asking? Or have I just assumed it's the same as an essay question I had on this subject a week or two ago?

When you feel confident that you have read and understood the question, then tackle it in just the same way as a coursework essay. Brainstorm for ideas, quickly note down your ideas, using either a list, a balloon diagram or a tree diagram (see pp. 80–85. Highlight the ideas you decide to use, group them and order them.

Look at your list or diagram to see how many main topics you are going to include in your essay. If you only find two, that's probably not enough. If you find twelve, that's probably too many. If you have, say, forty minutes to write an essay, four or five topics should be about right. Make a quick estimate of how much time you can give to each topic. Four topics in forty minutes, allowing some time for thinking and for writing an introduction and conclusion, gives you about eight minutes to a topic.

As you work through the essay, keep an eye on the time to see if you are spending too long on each topic. If so, you need to find a way to speed up a bit. Perhaps you could drop one of the topics or give less detail. If you do drop a topic, go back to the introduction to your essay, where – I hope – you will have signposted this topic, and cross out the signpost.

If you find that you have not left yourself enough time to deal properly with the *last* question on the paper, answer this question, however briefly, in note form. This will ensure that you get some marks for the question. However, do remember that the examiner will *not* be familiar with your particular note-taking habits, so it's no good using your usual abbreviations and signs or using a complicated note-taking format. Simply list your notes in a clear way.

For example, if you were writing notes on the topic of how tutors could help dyslexic students, you could simply write down your initial skeletal structure of this essay:

Organisation   Advise me on time management.

Help me organise a revision schedule.

Reading   Don't ask me to read out loud.

Star important items on reading lists.

Writing   Don't be hard on spelling.

Explain how to structure essays.

If you have to answer multiple-choice questions, read each question and possible answers *very carefully* before selecting the answer code. If your answer options are in a grid, use a ruler to keep your place in the grid. Initially, always use a pencil to mark the codes you select.

If there are, say, four possible answers to a question, put a cross in pencil against any answers you *know* are incorrect. Then you won't have to keep rereading these.

When you're sure about your answers, mark the correct ones in ink. Be sure to mark your chosen code clearly, and in exactly the right place, so that there can be no doubt about which code you have marked.

You may find it helpful to take a copy of the above advice into the examination with you. Check with the invigilator that this is allowed.

USEFUL TIP!

If you find writing arduous, use speech-to-text software and let the computer do the work for you.

For more information, see p. 196.

Writing at the postgraduate level

Writing at the postgraduate level is not, in essence, different from writing at the undergraduate level. A thesis, or dissertation, is like an extra long essay: you need to apply exactly the same principles of researching, note-taking and structuring your work as you did for an essay of normal length. In other words: identify the main topics you intend to write about; divide these, as appropriate, into sub-topics; decide the order in which you will deal with your material; and start writing.

If you think about a doctoral thesis as a whole, writing it could seem like a gargantuan task, but, if you break it down into sections and concentrate on one section at a time, you will find it quite manageable.

As you work on your thesis, you may find that your plans for it change as you go along. You might find some interesting avenues to explore which you hadn't originally thought of. Other avenues that you had thought of might turn out to be dead ends. But it's much easier to change the structure of the thesis as you go along, if, at the beginning, you started off with a clear structure. If you're in a muddle to begin with, then chopping and changing later on will just create more muddle. Start clear, stay clear. Don't be afraid to change your mind, but be clear what the changes are.

You may find that the subject you have chosen for your thesis is much broader and more complicated than you originally realised and that you have much more to say about it than you had anticipated. But remember: you don't have to put *everything* you know about a subject into your thesis – you just need to include enough to make the thesis viable. If you have interesting material left over, you can use this to write journal articles – and earn yourself some academic brownie points in the process.

This chapter and the previous four chapters are perhaps the most difficult ones in this book to absorb. They have necessarily been full of detailed advice on how to improve your skills. I suggest that you take time to read them over again, not all on the same day but perhaps at the rate of one chapter a week, and that you continually try to practise the strategies that they recommend. You will be glad to hear that the remaining chapters in the book will be an easier read.

Summary

In this chapter, you learnt how to:

- research and write an essay;
- write a scientific report;
- write in examinations;
- write a thesis or dissertation.

Chapter 9

Dyspraxia in focus

As was noted earlier in the book (Chapter 2), dyslexia and dyspraxia are on a continuum of difficulties, and, therefore, all the advice so far given in this book should be helpful to both dyspraxic and dyslexic students. However, as dyspraxia is generally less well understood than dyslexia, it will be useful to devote a chapter specifically to this topic. I'll begin by reminding you of the main areas of dyspraxic difficulty, and then look in detail at strategies for dealing with these difficulties. I'll also give advice on assessment, and on other conditions which may be associated with dyspraxia.

The four main areas of difficulty are:

- spatial skills;
- motor skills;
- organisational skills;
- social skills.

Spatial skills

Spatial skills are essentially the ability to judge distance and space. They are linked to spatial awareness, which is our ability to know where we are in relation to our surroundings.

It is possible to have one of these abilities more well-developed than the other. For example, a person may have good spatial judgment, and be able to, say, thread a needle with ease. Yet that same person may have little awareness of their own body and the space in which it moves; they may live 'in their heads' and take little heed of their physical surroundings.

Dyspraxic people, in particular, often report that they move through the world in a sort of spatial blur; they feel confused in noisy or complex environments, such as crowded streets or railway stations. Jim, a dyspraxic student, describes his difficulties as follows:

> I would describe myself as being permanently lost. Even going from my digs to college, a journey I make every day, I can take a wrong turning. Also, I often forget where I've left my bicycle, and spend ages wandering round the streets looking for it – and then I get lost myself as well.
>
> I can get into quite a state. Last week I was at the railway station to meet a friend, and I couldn't find the platform I needed. It seems ridiculous, but I suddenly panicked – there was a lot of noise everywhere, the loudspeaker announcements, train noises, people shouting. I felt sort of paralysed – the whole station seemed to be coming down on top of me.

It's not unusual for people to panic when they completely lose their bearings. Jim suddenly felt he was in danger, almost as if he were lost in a trackless jungle rather than just an everyday railway station. But the fact is that, as far as our body chemistry is concerned, panic is panic, and it makes little difference whether it overtakes you in a jungle or a station. Your body goes into the fight/flight response. As there is no one for you to fight, you may just stand paralysed – or if you decide to fly, you might rush blindly off in any direction.

To deal with such situations, you need to have strategies to calm yourself down. Don't try to do anything, but remain where you are and allow yourself to feel the panic. Try to breathe slowly and deeply. It may help to close your eyes; if not, focus on a particular object in your environment and look steadily at that. In the absence of prowling lions or poisonous snakes, the panic will die down in a few minutes. It won't do you any physical harm. The less notice you take of it, the more quickly it will go away. So try not to panic about panicking. And don't feel bad about yourself because you're prone to panicking in certain situations.

If, like Jim, you constantly forget which routes you have taken, and can't remember where you have parked your bicycle or car, get into the habit of noticing street names or landmarks along your route (e.g., Italian café on corner). You can text street names into your mobile phone, or speak them into a voice recorder as you go along. But – don't forget that right turns on your outward journey will be left turns on your return journey, and vice versa. Before you turn out of one street into another, turn round and look back for a moment at the way you have come. Then you will have a picture of your homeward route in your mind, and this will help you on your return journey. You could also consider buying a satellite navigation system.

One way to feel more at home in your physical surroundings is to feel more at home in your own body. If you feel 'grounded' physically, then you have a safe and secure base from which to observe the outside world. Below is a short body awareness exercise which you might like to incorporate into your weekly routine.

BODY AWARENESS EXERCISE

Lie comfortably on the floor with your head resting on a book or a flat cushion. Place your arms in any position which is comfortable for you.

Close your eyes and focus your attention on your body. Feel which parts of you are in contact with the floor, and notice the slight feeling of pressure this causes. Feel which parts of you are in contact with other parts of you. For example, perhaps you have your hands resting on your chest. If so, press your hands very gently against your chest, and then release the pressure. Do this a few times.

I want you now to imagine that you can feel a lovely warm sensation across the soles of your feet. This sensation is so lovely that you want it to fill your whole body. So you are gradually going to pull this sensation up like a warm stream through your body, making sure that you don't miss out even a fingertip. And as the stream reaches each part of your body, you will focus your attention on that particular part and fully recognise it as a part of yourself.

So bring the sensation first into the rest of your feet, and then gradually up your legs and into your torso. Then let it spread up through your abdomen, around your buttocks, up into your chest and across your upper back. From there, send it through your shoulders and down into your arms and hands right to the tips of your fingers. Leaving it there, return to your shoulders and finally push the sensation right up through your neck and into your head.

When you are wholly filled with this sensation, lie quietly for a few moments feeling its warm stream not only filling every part of you, but also *connecting* every part of you in a unified whole.

While you are lying quietly, you may become aware that your body is more than a passive recipient of sensations. It is in fact an alive body, a breathing body. So in the last part of this exercise, focus your attention on your breathing. Don't strain to breathe in any particular way; just observe the rhythm of your in-breaths and out-breaths and feel the connection which breathing makes between you and the world around you.

When you are ready to end the exercise, *don't move abruptly*. Stretch a little, bend your knees, sit up slowly and bring yourself gradually and fully into your environment. Stand up in a graceful easy way.

This exercise should take between fifteen and twenty minutes. However, please note that you don't need to be actually doing an exercise to practise body awareness. There are many moments in everyday life – waiting for an egg to boil, standing in the supermarket queue, sitting on a bus – when you could spend some quality time with your body.

Motor skills

Motor skills are the ability to plan and execute movement. In practice, motor skills are very much bound up with spatial skills, as, in order to make a movement, we have to judge the amount of space needed for the movement to be successfully performed. In this section, however, we will concentrate solely on the motor aspects of actions.

Two types of motor skills are generally distinguished:

- fine motor skills, which we need for tasks such as sewing, handwriting or using scissors;
- gross motor skills, which we need for tasks in which we make large movements, such as playing sports or walking up and down stairs.

If you feel that you have difficulties of either or both of these types, then you might like to consider having a formal assessment.

If your motor difficulties are so severe that they cause you problems in everyday life – for example, with cooking, dressing, shaving or using keys – then you could seek an assessment from an occupational therapist. The therapist would be able to give you better strategies for doing practical tasks. Such an assessment could be arranged through your GP or through the college medical centre. You might also qualify for the Disability Living Allowance which provides funds for a personal helper and for specialist equipment.

For a general assessment of dyslexic and dyspraxic difficulties which will be more related to problems with study, you will need to see a chartered psychologist or specialist dyslexia tutor *who is qualified to assess both dyslexia and dyspraxia.*

You could also put your own creative talent to work and think of strategies which might help you in particular situations. Here, a dyspraxic student, Ben, describes how he 'cured' himself of walking into door frames or open doors.

I'm always bumping into things, especially doors, and I'm never without a bruise somewhere or other. Even though I consciously try to aim for the middle of the doorway, I seem to finish up either tripping over the open door or crashing into the door frame.

I solved this problem by sticking two brightly coloured markers on the floor, each about six inches from one side of the door. Now I aim for the space between the markers, and this usually keeps me out of trouble. Also, this has somehow helped me judge other doorways and spaces where I can't put stickers.

USEFUL TIP !

If you have difficulty with manual tasks such as opening tins or turning knobs, you can get a wide variety of helpful gadgets from disability organisations. See page 207 for more information.

You could also take steps to make the physical act of writing or typing easier. The discomfort which often accompanies these activities usually stems from a combination of bad posture and poor fine motor skills. So it is important, whenever possible, to write or type at a table of a comfortable height, and to have a chair that supports your back. If possible, use an ergonomic keyboard: this will both improve your posture and take the strain off your hands and arms. Wrist rests and mouse pads with wrist support are also helpful.

Working on a laptop can cause particular discomfort, because the keys are small and close together, and therefore your hands have to operate within an unnaturally restricted range of movement. You could solve this problem by using a full-sized wireless keyboard and mouse.

Organisational skills

Dyspraxic people frequently report that they have poor organisational skills. They feel they live in a permanent chaos of lost possessions, muddled working practices, missed deadlines and forgotten appointments. They find it hard to sequence their ideas logically when they are speaking or writing, and they can easily lose the logical thread of what someone else is saying to them. They may find it hard to transfer ideas or knowledge from one situation to another, for example, to apply their theoretical knowledge of a subject to its practical application.

Organisational skills are in fact important in almost every aspect of our lives. Already in this book, we have looked at general work organisation (Chapter 4) and ways of structuring written work (Chapter 8). In this chapter I'll deal with speaking and listening skills.

Speaking and listening

In order to speak clearly, you need to be clear in your own mind about what you want to say. You also need to be clear about what you *need* to say, i.e., how much your listener needs or wants to know.

These two things may be very different. Suppose someone asks you what dyspraxia is. You may be very well-informed on this subject, but in formulating your reply you need to consider two things: (a) how you can express your knowledge in a clear and succinct way, and (b) how much knowledge you can expect your listener to take in. Are they making a casual inquiry out of politeness? Or are they perhaps wondering if they are dyspraxic and want to get some detailed knowledge of the subject? Speaking without considering the needs of your listener is not communication. (More on this in the next section, on social skills.)

In a social situation it is impossible to know what topics of conversation might come up, and so it's difficult to plan in advance what you want to say. There might, however, be some things that you *hope* to talk about, and you could think through these beforehand. And in formal situations – such as interviews, seminars, tutorials, meetings – you could make some advance notes for yourself. Look back to pages 104–5 to remind yourself how to prepare for seminar presentations.

As with speaking, so with listening: there are informal situations which may leave you floundering. One way in which you can focus better on what someone is saying is to keep your gaze on the speaker. If your gaze wanders round the room, you are more likely to be distracted. In formal situations, such as lectures or meetings, you can take notes or record the proceedings. Advice on note-taking has been given in Chapter 6.

PROBLEMS AND SOLUTIONS

Alison, Psychology student
I was having difficulty following verbal instructions from my tutor, particularly about how to set up experiments, so I asked her to either e-mail instructions to me, or allow me to record them. This made life easier for both of us!

Terry, Computer Studies student
I can work out a problem on the computer, but find it hard to explain to my tutor just how I've done it. I try to go through the process in a step-by-step way, but usually get muddled. Then I start panicking, which make things worse.

Now I've found a way round this problem. Before speaking to my tutor, I work through the process in my own mind, and write down some 'connecting' phrases, such as:

> Firstly
> Next
> Two possible ways forward at this point
> I chose
> The reason was
> etc
>
> This helps me to give a clear explanation of what I did and why. And if I do lose my way while I'm speaking, my tutor can look at my notes and get me back on track.

Social skills

As noted earlier in the book (Chapter 2), we live not just in a physical space, but also – metaphorically speaking – in a social space. In physical space, we need to judge how far away we are, for instance, from a door frame; in social space, we need to judge the best way to share the space with another person. Social skills are the ability to make this latter judgment correctly.

In making this judgment, we need to take into account a great number of things: how much we should speak, in what tone we should speak, what we should talk about, at what physical distance we should place ourselves from the other person, what signals they are giving us, verbally or non-verbally, and, likewise, what signals we might be giving them.

Rather than expand on this topic in the abstract, I'm going to illustrate good and bad social skills respectively by describing two imagined encounters between a young man called Jack and a young woman

called Jill. Please focus particularly on Jack's
behaviour.

Encounter 1

Jack is walking along a country lane carrying a bucket.
He meets a neighbour, Jill.

Jack (*smiling*):   Hi there – how are you? Haven't
                       seen you for ages.

Jill (*also smiling*): Hi – I'm fine – but very busy. Choir
                       practice every day at the moment.

Jack: Oh – are you doing a concert?

Jill: Yes, this weekend at the cathedral.

Jack: Good luck with it!

Jill: Thanks – anyway, how are *you*?

Jack: Not brilliant today actually – mega
                       problems with the plumbing. We've
                       got no water so I'm going up to the
                       spring to get some.

Jill: Ah – I wondered why you were
                       carrying a bucket.

(*They both laugh, and then there is a short pause.*)

Jack: Er – are you just coming back from
                       choir practice now?

Jill: Yes, just on my way home.

Jack: Have you got any plans for the rest
                       of the day?

Jill (*blushing slightly*):
                       No, nothing in particular.

Jack: Well, why don't you come up to the
                       spring with me so we can chat
                       a bit?

Jill (*looking doubtfully at the hill*):

> Well, I'm not sure – the hill's a bit steep on this side. Isn't it dangerous?

Jack:

> No – don't worry – I know an easy way up.

Jill (*smiling*):   Oh, all right then!

(*They set off together towards the hill.*)

From this encounter, one might conclude that Jack's sense of danger was somewhat lacking, but his social skills were excellent. Although he appears to be the dominant partner in the conversation, being perhaps less shy than Jill, he does not in any way 'hog' the social space between them. Note in particular that:

- He does not speak at length, but continually pauses for Jill to reply. Thus the amount of speaking that each does is approximately equal.
- At the beginning of the encounter, he says, 'Haven't seen you for ages'. This contains a slight suggestion that he has missed seeing Jill. If so, he has managed to express this in a subtle way which will not embarrass her.
- When Jill mentions something that she is doing, i.e., choir practice, Jack asks her more about it.
- When asked how he is, he explains his situation briefly, not burdening Jill with detail.
- Before asking Jill to accompany him to the spring, he 'tests the waters' by asking her if she is busy that day, and no doubt he notices her blushing, which seems like a sign of interest on her part.

Outlook for this relationship: promising.

Now compare this with a different version of Jack in:

Encounter 2

Jack is walking along a country lane carrying a bucket.
He meets a neighbour, Jill.

Jack:	Hi there – where are you off to?
Jill:	Just going back home – from yet another choir practice. (*Slight pause*) So, how are things with you?
Jack:	Not brilliant today actually – mega problems with the plumbing. We've got no water so I'm going up to the spring to get some.
Jill:	Ah – I wondered why you were carrying a bucket.
Jack:	Well, you just wouldn't believe the problems we've had. I've been trying to get a plumber since yesterday morning. I phoned that one who lives in the village – you know that one just by the church. Larry something or other. He said he'd come at 2 o'clock, and at five o'clock there was still no sign of him.
Jill:	Well, perhaps he . . .

Jack:	So I went round to his house, and he was just sitting in the garden smoking. His girl-friend was there too – you know – that girl who used to live at Fletcher's farm before she got a job in the school – the one that got sacked for stealing the dinner money?
Jill (*stifling a yawn*):	No, I don't know her.
Jack:	Well, anyway, he promised to come this morning, but he still hasn't turned up.
Jill (*preparing to move away*):	
	Well, I hope he will.
Jack:	Hey – do you feel like a walk? Come up to the spring with me.
Jill (*looking away*):	No – sorry! That hill's too steep for me.
Jack (*grasping her arm*):	Don't worry – I'll help you.
Jill (*pulling away*):	Sorry, must go.

(*Jack sets off towards the hill and Jill heads for home.*)

In this encounter Jack's social skills are abysmal. He takes up almost all of the social space, confining Jill to a small corner of the conversation. Note in particular that:

- When he first speaks to Jill, he doesn't ask her how she is, but rather intrusively 'demands' to know where she is going.

- When she mentions the choir, he takes no interest.
- When describing his difficulties with the plumber, he goes into unnecessary detail.
- He also goes off at a tangent by talking about the plumber's girlfriend.
- When Jill attempts to say something, he interrupts her and carries on with his story.
- He fails to notice all the non-verbal signals Jill is giving that she is bored: stifling a yawn, trying to move away.
- He ignores her definite statement that she does not want to ascend the hill.
- He intrudes into her physical space by grasping her arm, forcing her to wrench herself free.

Outlook for this relationship: bleak.

A harsh judgment on this second Jack would be that he is a selfish and unpleasant character. A more charitable judgment would be that he simply has no concept of social skills. If he were able to learn better social habits from his more congenial namesake, then perhaps his overtures to Jill would be more welcome.

If you yourself feel that you need to develop better social skills, you need to begin by getting a clear picture of what your present habits are, and then take steps to change them. So you will need to do the following three things:

> Observe
> Analyse
> Modify

The processes of observing and analysing have already been illustrated in the Jack and Jill stories. We began by observing exactly what happened in these encounters, and then analysed why one encounter went well, and the other badly.

You need to do exactly the same thing with your own behaviour. Of course, you can't go round tape-recording your conversations with people, but you can reflect at leisure on conversations you have had. Go through in your mind the course a conversation took, and try to analyse why it went well or badly.

If it went badly, was this your fault, or was the other person difficult? If you think it was your fault, where did you go wrong? Did you talk too much? Too loudly? Or did you fail to make adequate responses to what the other person was saying? Were you even really aware that another person was present, or were you totally bound up in your own concerns?

Having observed and analysed your behaviour, you may decide that you want to modify it. Let's say, for example, that you feel you are in the habit of talking too much. How can you stop yourself doing this?

It is not enough to be aware, in the abstract, that this is a bad habit, you now need to maintain this awareness *at the time you are engaging in a conversation.* Then you can take steps to alter your behaviour during the conversation. So keep a sharp eye on yourself when you are conversing with someone. Some people like to imagine this observational side of themselves as a separate person, a sort of mentor, who will give you a nudge when you are talking too much.

In order to bring yourself suddenly to a stop when you are in full flow, you might need to openly acknowledge your problem. For instance, you can say: 'Oh sorry, I'm getting lost in detail – the main point is . . .' or 'Sorry, I've gone off at a tangent again – the important thing is . . .'

In general, you could try to be more careful about leaving space for the other person to talk. For instance, you could bring them into the conversation by asking them for their opinion, rather than simply telling them yours.

Changing ingrained habits is not easy, but if you cultivate an awareness of how you are behaving, and actively devise strategies for altering bad habits, then you should gradually be able to bring about change. You might like to keep a 'log' of your progress.

In this chapter we've looked at a number of dyspraxic difficulties, as it were, in isolation. However, as noted above, dyspraxic difficulties are on a continuum with dyslexic difficulties, and many people have a mixture of both. And moving along this same continuum beyond dyspraxia, we come to two further sets of difficulties: Attention Deficit Disorder (ADD) and Asperger's Syndrome.

ADD, as its name implies, denotes difficulties with attention and concentration, and often also has a component of impulsive behaviour. Asperger's Syndrome denotes a difficulty in relating to people not just socially, but also on the emotional level. One or other of these two syndromes may co-occur with dyspraxia, and so a support organisation, DANDA, has been formed which can offer advice on all three of these syndromes. Also, DANDA publishes a useful booklet called *Living with Dyspraxia*. For more information see pages 206–7 and 213.

Summary

In this chapter advice has been given on:

- finding one's way about in unfamiliar surroundings;
- dealing with panic;
- developing body awareness;
- coping with clumsiness;
- arranging a dyspraxia assessment;
- organising one's thoughts when speaking;
- following what other people are saying;
- improving social skills;
- ADD and Asperger's Syndrome.

Chapter 10

Ways of feeling

In the first chapter of this book, you made the acquaintance of Clare, the dyslexic psychology student who found her first weeks at college something of a nightmare. As you may recall, Clare managed to overcome her problems and went on to do a postgraduate course in neuro-psychology.

During her postgraduate years, Clare added another string to her bow: she decided to become an adviser to dyslexic and dyspraxic students and, over a three-year period, saw a large number of students of all ages – from twenty-somethings to seventy-somethings.

In this chapter – with the generous permission of Clare and several of her clients – I have reproduced material from these counselling sessions in written form. In other words, I have transformed Clare into a dyslexia 'agony aunt'. In the letters that follow, the names of the students concerned have been changed.

I just feel confused . . .

Dear Clare,

I'm writing to see if you can help me a bit with some confusion I have about dyslexia. I've known that I'm dyslexic for as long as I can remember – I used to get extra help at school with reading and writing. When I started at college, I had to get an up-to-date assessment, but I find I can't really understand what the results of this mean.

The psychologist's report mentions all sorts of problems, not just reading and writing but things like memory and organisation and what she calls spatial problems. What's worrying me is that I feel if I have so many problems should I really be at college? Am I setting myself up for failure? The psychologist told me that I did have good general abilities and that I should be able to complete my degree with help, but I can't really make sense of it all: how can my general abilities be good when so many things are wrong?

For instance, in my everyday life, lots of things happen that make me feel like a complete idiot – sometimes I just don't follow what people are saying to me, or I can't get my thoughts in order when I'm trying to speak to someone. But then, at other times, I seem to catch on to things quicker than other people. Basically, I just feel confused about what it all means, and I never feel confident about myself. In any given situation I never know if I'll make a good impression or fall flat on my face. Can you help me make any sense of all this?

Dear Andrew,

Thank you for your letter, in which you express worries and concerns which many dyslexic students have. I think one reason why dyslexia is so baffling is that it is, by definition, a mixture of strengths and weaknesses. Someone has described it as a series of 'unexpected failings'.

A second reason is that it's not immediately obvious what link there is between these various 'failings'. I would have hoped that your assessor explained to you that there are certain basic dyslexic weaknesses, e.g., in memory and perception, and that most of the 'failings' arise out of these in one way or another.

For example, poor memory can cause you difficulty with remembering names, pronouncing long words, following what people say and organising your own thoughts when you're speaking to people.

Once you have identified the underlying difficulties and how they affect both your studies and everyday life, then you can focus attention on getting better skills and strategies to deal with them. And then you can narrow the gap between your strengths and your weaknesses.

You say that you lack confidence in yourself at present. But I think that when you have a better understanding of your difficulties, and better strategies in place to deal with them, you will feel much more confident and more aware of your strengths. So you need to read a bit more about dyslexia and take full advantage of the specialist tuition which will be offered to you at college. You should then find that things become a lot easier.

I wish you every success.

I felt so angry . . .

Dear Clare,

I'm a third-year politics student and have both dyslexic and dyspraxic problems. I can just about cope with my work, but it takes me hours and hours to do things. I'm often slaving away till midnight while my flatmates have knocked off at eight and have gone over to the bar. I get very tired and very frustrated. What makes me really angry is that other people don't show any understanding of my difficulties. My flatmates seem to think they're a bit of a joke, and I have one particular tutor who's completely unsympathetic. When I tried to speak to him about the problems I was having, particularly with reading, he just said, well, being at college isn't all about pubbing and clubbing – you do have to knuckle down and do some work sometimes.

All this makes me feel quite isolated. I seem to spend my time either working, sleeping or falling out with people. For instance, the other day, I got lost in one of the college buildings – that's

continued on next page

something that often happens to me – and by accident I found myself in a 'staff only' area. Someone came out of an office and started telling me off. I felt so angry that he couldn't be just a bit helpful that I swore at him. It was a spur-of-the-moment thing – I'm not usually like that. But anyway, a few days later, I received a warning note from the college saying that I could be suspended if I repeated this type of threatening behaviour towards staff. I feel I need sympathy and help, not threats, but don't really know where to turn.

Dear David,

I'm sorry to hear about the difficulties you're having and quite understand that you feel both fatigued and frustrated.

The first thing to say is that, however much work you have to get through, it is not useful to go slogging on hour after hour without a break. Try to stick to a routine of working for, say, three-quarters of an hour and then taking a quarter of an hour's break. Also, try to give yourself at least a couple of hours off each evening for leisure activities.

You obviously have a lot of frustration and anger built up inside you, and it is easy for this to spill out onto somebody else, especially someone who shows no understanding of your difficulties. One thing you could do after a distressing incident like the one you mention is to put aside your annoyance – however justified – with the other person and to think how *you* might have behaved differently in the situation. Could you have used the energy of your anger in a more useful way than swearing at the person – and inevitably making the situation worse? Could you have behaved in a way which might prompt the other person to modify *their* behaviour and be more helpful?

The fact is that most people you meet will have no idea about dyslexia and the different problems it causes. And even if they do know about dyslexia, they will have no way of knowing that you are dyslexic. So, in a situation where your behaviour is misinterpreted, you could try to contain your anger and put your energy instead into 'putting the other person right' in a firm but courteous way.

Would the situation have evolved differently, do you think, if you had dealt with it assertively rather than angrily, if you had said, for instance, 'I'm very sorry, but I have dyslexic difficulties, and I do tend to get lost. Could you kindly directly me to' . . .?

I'm wondering, too, whether some of your anger is really directed against yourself rather than other people, whether you are angry about your own inefficiencies. If so, may I suggest that you treat yourself with much more kindness: why beat up the very parts of yourself which you feel to be weak? Try to look upon them with more tender eyes . . .

If you do continue to be prone to angry outbursts, you could check in with the student health service and ask to speak to one of the psychologists there. They run anger-management programmes, and you might find these very useful.

I don't feel I'm disabled . . .

Dear Clare,

I'm writing to ask why dyslexic students are given the label 'disabled'. I've always had dyslexic difficulties, but I find ways of dealing with them and I don't feel I'm disabled. When I came up to the college, I was surprised to find I had to apply for a Disabled Students Allowance. It makes me feel as if I've got some huge problems. In fact I think that my dyslexia has quite a few advantages that more than balance the difficulties. For example, I often feel I can grasp things quite quickly and intuitively and can often find creative solutions to things, while my non-dyslexic friends are sort of plodding along, taking a long time to come up with answers. I'm doing art and design, which is something I think I've really got a flair for. I didn't choose law because I knew that would be difficult for me. So where's the problem? A lot of law students would be hopeless at art and design, but nobody calls them disabled.

Dear Rosemary,

Good point! Perhaps the Disabled Students Allowance should be called the enabled students allowance. I know that many students feel rather surprised to find themselves suddenly put into the disabled category. However, other students who have quite severe difficulties do actually feel disabled and so are not affronted by the label.

You'll find that when you leave college and enter employment, you will come up against this same difficulty, because dyslexic people who request help and support in the workplace invoke the protection of a piece of legislation called the Disability Discrimination Act.

Whatever the label, the fact is that the current disability legislation is a very good deal for dyslexic people, because it makes available very substantial sums of money to pay for any help and support that is needed. I don't suppose the powers that be will consider creating a new bit of legislation called the different students allowance, so I suggest that what you should do is simply bite the bullet on this.

I seem to feel anxious all the time . . .

Hello Clare,

I'm in my second year doing a physics degree. The particular worry I'm writing to you about is that I seem to feel anxious all the time, anxious about things like not getting through the reading or just generally not keeping up with work.

Recently, I've felt this anxiety has got worse, and I've suffered what I think are panic attacks.

continued on next page

The first time this happened was in one of my end-of-year exams. I had done a lot of revision, but when I got into the exam and looked at the questions, I felt a sudden panic that I couldn't do any of them. I started to feel funny, my heart was thumping horribly and I felt a bit faint.

The examiner came up and asked me if I felt all right, and I said I felt ill. So they let me go out for a while, and I sat in the loo for about twenty minutes with an invigilator making sure I wasn't cheating! It was really embarrassing. Anyway, after I calmed down a bit I went back into the exam. When I looked at the questions again, I saw that there were questions that I could do, but because I'd lost time at the beginning of the exam, I didn't finish the paper.

I also get very panicky in seminars. I want to contribute to the seminar, but just the thought of speaking out sets off another panic, so I usually just sit there saying nothing. It all seems to be getting worse, and I'm not sure what to do.

Dear Jenny,

Panic attacks are very common, and they do feel absolutely awful at the time. The first thing to say about them is that, however dreadful they feel, they do not actually do you any physical harm. Your body has temporarily got into an agitated state, but it can't maintain this level of agitation in the absence of any real threat, so you will find that the attack will eventually die away of its own accord, as it did in your sitting-in-the-loo experience.

Panic attacks do feed on themselves: once you've had one, it's very easy to have another. That's because you're not only fearing an actual situation, such as doing an exam, but also, on top of this, you're fearing having another panic attack. So you can get into a cycle of panic attacks which recur long after you've left the original frightening experience behind. In order to deal with this problem, you have to somehow intervene in this cycle of ever-spiralling panic. You have to find some way of sending a message to your body that these panic attacks are pointless and need to be discouraged.

The best way to go about this is to develop some physical and mental relaxation routines which you practise on a regular basis and which you can summon to your aid if a panic attack threatens or if you just start feeling anxious. You can buy tapes which will guide you through muscle relaxation and meditation exercises. Breathing exercises are also very beneficial as you can practise these even in public places.

If you do want to start speaking out in seminars, the best way to do this – paradoxically – might be to offer to make a presentation rather than just try to make a few remarks now and again. The reason is that, however bad you feel at the beginning of your presentation, your panic will gradually die down as you continue speaking, and so, if you can keep going, you will eventually enjoy the experience of speaking without panic. This will reduce the likelihood of your panicking the next time you speak. If, however, you confine yourself to brief remarks, made in a state of panic, or never risk speaking at all, you will remain a prisoner of the panic.

If possible, speak to your tutor and fellow students about your difficulties in seminars so that they can make due allowance and give you encouragement. Don't keep the panic as a 'guilty secret'. Ten to one, if you go public with your panic, other people around you will also admit that they too have panicky feelings on occasion.

I strongly recommend that you also seek help from a behavioural psychologist at the student health centre. He or she will be able to give you training in panic-reduction techniques.

There were so many missed opportunities . . .

Dear Clare,

I'm in my mid-forties and have just begun an English degree. It took a bit of courage to attempt this, because I don't have any experience in doing academic work. I left school at the age of fifteen with no qualifications – always had a lot of trouble at school with reading and writing, and was put in the 'no-hopers' group and not really taught anything. This was frustrating, because I really wanted to learn. After school, I had various jobs, mainly manual or in retail, but I had a lot of difficulty holding down a job as I was always in trouble for getting things wrong.

Also, I tried to do courses at various times to get some qualifications, but I always found the work too difficult. What's prompted me now to try for a degree is that my wife was recently reading about dyslexia and thought that this may have been my problem all along. It seemed that I might get some help for my difficulties at college, so I thought I would give it a try.

I was assessed for dyslexia in my first term and told that I did have moderately severe difficulties. This came as something of a shock. It suddenly seemed as if there had been something obvious in my life which I had never seen or realised and that if I had realised it, things might have been very different.

When the shock wore off, I actually started to feel quite angry about this and then also quite depressed, because there were so many missed opportunities, so many frustrations at work and years of feeling a miserable failure.

I saw a notice about a dyslexia support group at college and decided to attend it, but I found it the very opposite of support. Most of the people there were much younger than me, and I was immediately aware that they had a much more positive attitude towards their dyslexia than I did.

continued on next page

I made an attempt to explain what had happened to me, and how I felt about all the lost years, as I felt them to be. But at this point, the group leader reacted by telling me that I was seeing things in much too negative a light and that really my dyslexia was a gift and I should be grateful for it. I was so angry I just got up and walked out. How can forty years of frustration and despair and lost opportunities be called a gift?

Dear William,

I do understand your feelings, and they are, of course, justified. I think the group leader's remark was insensitive, though I can understand that what she said was genuinely true for her. You, however, are not her – you have a different life experience, and a different experience of dyslexia.

The way people feel about their dyslexic difficulties does differ widely. A lot depends on the severity of the problems, how early the dyslexia has been recognised and how much help has been given. These days, dyslexia is often picked up quite early, at school or at college, and there is a general positive feeling about it – it's not regarded, as it used to be, as some sort of stigma or failure, and there is an expectation that the difficulties can be successfully managed.

However, for people in your age group or older, the experience is generally very different. In most cases, your difficulties have never been recognised, you have been regarded, as you say, as a 'no-hoper', and you have never received any appropriate help. Your efforts to further your education and to progress in your working life have been thwarted. The emotions you feel about all this are painful ones: frustration, anxiety, bafflement, anger and despondency, even despair. So I can quite understand that, if a person breezes up to you and cheerfully pronounces your dyslexia to be a gift, then you will quite probably want to strangle them.

Perhaps you could turn for support instead to a professional counsellor (available at the student health centre) who will be more focused on discussing your actual feelings and how to deal with them rather than taking a particular line about what dyslexia is or is not.

It seems to me that, at present, you are in the throes of a classic bereavement syndrome. Before your assessment, your life was difficult, but you didn't have a clear idea about how it might be different. After the assessment, when the situation was explained to you, you came to feel that you had actually *lost* half your life, and so a grief reaction was natural. There are usually four stages to the grieving process: the initial shock of realising something valuable has been lost, then anger about the loss, then a period of depression and, finally, a feeling of moving on from – though not forgetting – what has happened and looking to the future.

At present, you seem to be somewhere between anger and depression, but, given that you will now be getting help for your difficulties, I think that you will gradually come out of this distressing phase and feel able to move on. You may not be able to feel positive about your previous experiences of being dyslexic, but you may find you can become more positive about your dyslexic future. In the meantime, ignore well-meaning but inappropriate advice about being grateful for your dyslexia. You have a right to feel your own emotions, whether positive or negative. So, give the pain the space it needs, and then move on.

I blunder around in social situations . . .

Dear Clare,

I don't have dyslexic difficulties, but I am very dyspraxic – disorganised, always getting lost, spilling and dropping things. All this I can sort of cope with; what I feel is my main difficulty is relating to other people. I read in a book recently that people with dyspraxia are not only clumsy in the physical sense but also in the social sense. I feel this is true of me because I do blunder around in social situations, interrupting people, laughing at the wrong moments and talking too loud or too long. I have two close friends who seem to be able to see beyond my social difficulties, but I think most people find me difficult – they tend to edge away from me at parties. Problems in seminars too: I tend to interrupt the tutor before she's finished explaining something, or to go off at a tangent, and people get impatient with me. Is there some way I can get help with this?

Dear Mike,

Your description of dyspraxia is a very good one. It's not always realised that dyspraxic people have social difficulties as well as physical ones. One immediate thing you could do to help your situation is to take your tutor to one side and explain your difficulties so that she is better able to support you in a seminar.

As for trying to make your actual behaviour less socially clumsy, you should be able to get some help for this from a dyslexia tutor who is also knowledgeable about dyspraxia. The tutor could do exercises with you to improve your social skills. When you are arranging for tuition with the college's dyslexia support coordinator, be sure to stress that you need a tutor who knows how to help dyspraxic students.

If you feel your physical coordination difficulties are also a problem – as they might be, for instance, for science students who have to work with laboratory equipment – you could also discuss with the coordinator the possibility of getting some help from an occupational therapist.

As well as getting help at college, you could contact DANDA, the national organisation that supports dyspraxic adults, as they may know of local social-skills courses or support groups. See p. 206 for more details.

I don't think I'm a visual person . . .

Dear Clare,

I'm a postgraduate doing an MA in Biological Sciences. I've been getting help for my dyslexic difficulties and have been told that, as a dyslexic person, I will be good at 'right-brained' activities, which I gather means I should have good visual skills. Following this advice, I've been using some study-skills guides that present information very visually – drawings, diagrams, flow charts, etc.

The problem is that actually I don't think I am a very visual person. I find that looking at page after page of 'visuals' is quite tiring and confusing, and my brain just tends to switch off after a few pages.

Also, I recently found that I suffer from visual stress, and this apparently accounts for the fact that I often see lines as going blurry. Another piece of advice I've been given that doesn't work is that I should use a lot of colour coding. Actually, I find colours quite stressful, especially red and blue. They seem to 'flash' at me and to dance about, and it's all very disturbing and distracting.

It's a bit disheartening to find that I'm really bad at things that a dyslexic person is supposed to be good at. I don't feel I'm without talents: I'm a good scientist and quite a creative thinker, and I've got good practical abilities. But I don't seem to have this right-brained visual talent that people talk about. Where am I going wrong?

Dear Zoe,

Your letter serves as a cautionary tale. Generalisations about dyslexia can be misleading, and the idea that dyslexic difficulties always come twinned with visual talents is simplistic. Many dyslexic people, especially those who are also dyspraxic, have difficulty in analysing visual material and don't appreciate being told that this is one of their strengths.

The important thing is to find out which learning style best suits *you*. Some people do learn well using visual methods; others prefer material presented in a verbal sequential way; others prefer a mix of the two techniques. It may well be helpful to your concentration to use a variety of different approaches: page after page of visuals could, like page after page of text, become wearisome.

So, don't start off with an *assumption* that this or that will be best: try things out. Suppose, for example, that you want to develop an efficient note-taking technique. Can you really decide before trying out different techniques which one is going to suit you? If you start off by classifying yourself as right-brained, and confining yourself to making notes in a visual way, you may actually be putting unhelpful limits on yourself.

What is certain is that when you find which learning methods suit you best, you will find academic work less of a struggle, and you will be able to put more of your energy into areas where you can exercise your talents. And even if you have no particular spectacular talent, you will feel the benefit of this extra energy in everything that you do, however modest your achievements.

So, when it comes to learning styles, I can give you no better advice than the maxim which the ancient Greeks inscribed over their holiest of holies, the Temple to Apollo at Delphi:

KNOW YOURSELF!

I hope that you have found it helpful to read these letters; they present a representative sample of the type of problems which dyslexic and dyspraxic students regularly report. If you yourself feel that you have similar problems and are not managing to cope with them, don't hesitate to seek advice and help from one of the doctors or counsellors at the student health centre.

Part III

Significant others

Tutors and employers

Introduction

In this third section of the book, you will find a quick guide to dyslexia and dyspraxia which can photocopy and give to any of your tutors who are in need of it. There is also advice on career choice, how to deal with your dyslexic difficulties when you are applying for jobs and when you are actually in employment.

Chapter 11

Dyslexia and dyspraxia

A quick guide for subject tutors

If you teach in further education, higher education or on a professional training course, you will probably already have been approached by students who tell you that they have dyslexic or dyspraxic difficulties and that they need extra support. You may feel unclear about the exact nature of the problems experienced by these students and about what you can do to help.

In this chapter, I shall explain the nature of dyslexic/dyspraxic difficulties and how they affect study and then make suggestions as to how you can help students manage these difficulties during their course.

Dyslexia and dyspraxia

Dyslexic and dyspraxic difficulties are on a continuum, as you will see from the figure below, and, so, there is no clear dividing line between them.

Students with dyslexic difficulties would certainly have weaknesses in phonology and auditory memory. They would probably also have difficulty with the skills shown in the middle three shaded areas, but not necessarily with spatial and motor skills.

Sylvia Moody, *Dyslexia: Surviving and succeeding at college* (Oxon: Routledge, 2007).

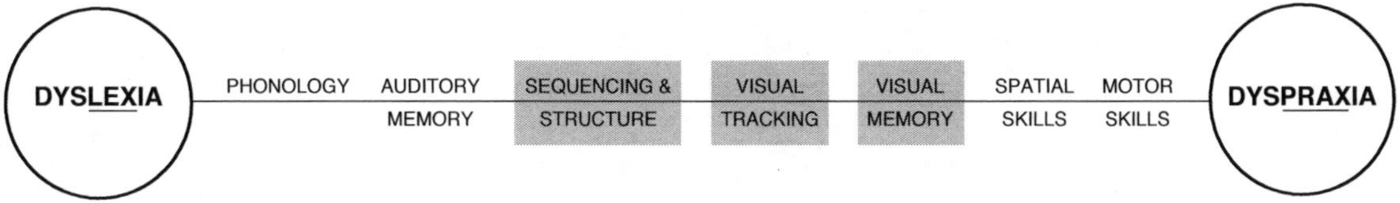

Figure 10.1 The dyslexia–dyspraxia continuum.

Students with dyspraxia would certainly have weaknesses in spatial and motor skills. They would probably also have difficulty with the skills shown in the middle three shaded areas, but not necessarily with auditory memory or phonology.

Most students will have a mixture of all these difficulties, and for convenience, in the rest of this chapter, I shall use the term 'dyslexia' to cover both dyslexia and dyspraxia.

Study problems

Table 10.1 shows the different elements of dyslexic difficulties and the study problems associated with each.

Table 10.1

Dyslexic difficulty	Associated study problems
Phonology (especially sequencing sounds)	• Accuracy in reading and spelling • Pronouncing long words • Slowness in reading
Auditory memory	• Following instructions and explanations • Note-taking in lectures • Reading comprehension
Sequencing and structure	• Structuring an essay • Speaking logically and succinctly • Organisational skills
Visual tracking	• Reading and spelling long words and numbers • Keeping place in page of text

continued on next page

Sylvia Moody, *Dyslexia: Surviving and succeeding at college* (Oxon: Routledge, 2007).

Visual memory	• Remembering irregular spellings • Recalling where things have been put • Remembering plans and diagrams
Spatial skills	• Dealing with data presented in charts, tables, graphs, etc. • Finding way about
Motor skills	• Poor handwriting • Clumsiness in handling laboratory equipment

Ways to help

Adopting a sympathetic attitude

The first step to adopting a sympathetic attitude is, of course, to inform yourself about the full range of dyslexic difficulties (as you are doing now). You will then be aware that one of the main characteristics of dyslexic students is that they tend to take longer than their non-dyslexic peers in doing things, whether this be reading, writing, understanding what is said to them or formulating their own thoughts. If you are a quick-thinking, rapid-talking sort of person, it is easy to feel impatient with a dyslexic student who seems to be lagging behind you all the time. However, any show of impatience is certain to make the situation worse, as it will make the student anxious, and the anxiety will in turn increase the student's difficulties.

You may need to be particularly sensitive to this difficulty in a seminar. A dyslexic student may feel nervous about speaking or perhaps begin to speak

Sylvia Moody, *Dyslexia: Surviving and succeeding at college* (Oxon: Routledge, 2007).

and then fluff what they're trying to say and dry up. So, some gentle encouragement to help them express their thoughts is helpful, rather than just passing on to another speaker. If you become aware that some dyslexic students never speak in a seminar, you might want to try to find ways to help them get started with this. Perhaps you could ask them to present a very short talk on a topic for just five minutes or so, and to practise this on you first.

An opposite problem can also occur. Dyslexic students can, through nervousness, talk too much: they may get involved in long rambling sentences from which it seems they may never emerge; or they may lose the thread of what they are saying. It may be clear that they have knowledge about the subject on which they are speaking but cannot present this knowledge in a succinct way. In this case, it can be useful to ask prompt questions so that students can present their material in a series of brief answers.

It's also important generally to keep an eye on dyslexic students to see how well they are keeping up with course requirements. Some students are articulate, even vociferous, about their difficulties, and will come and tell you if they feel overwhelmed with work. Other students, however, may simply retreat into themselves, feeling that they have to take responsibility for their difficulties and shouldn't keep asking for help. With such students, the danger is that their problems will go unrecognised until the situation reaches crisis point, and the student perhaps leaves the course.

Sylvia Moody, *Dyslexia: Surviving and succeeding at college* (Oxon: Routledge, 2007).

Most students will be getting help at some point from a dyslexia tutor and will be given IT support. However, this help is not usually available to the student at the time they start their course – it may be well into the second term before the relevant assessments have been done and provision made. Consequently, the first term is a critical period. A student who seems unable to cope during this period needs to be, as it were, held in suspension until appropriate help is available for them – at which point, their coping strategies may become adequate.

Reading

One of the main problems which dyslexic students face is the large amount of reading they have to do. So, if you give your students a reading list, it is useful to have a starring system for the items to indicate which books or articles are the most valuable or urgent to read. It's also useful to draw the attention of students to review articles, so that they can get an overview of their subject. It is not advisable to ask dyslexic students to read out loud at any time, unless they have explicitly said that they feel comfortable with this.

Also, be aware that dyslexic students may have difficulty in quickly reading things you've written down on a blackboard or whiteboard. If possible, use an interactive whiteboard.

Sylvia Moody, *Dyslexia: Surviving and succeeding at college* (Oxon: Routledge, 2007).

Absorbing information

If students need to copy down, or take from your dictation, instructions for essay topics or other course requirements, don't assume that dyslexic students will have taken these down correctly. It's always best to give them instructions in writing, if possible. When talking to dyslexic students, try to speak fairly slowly, to repeat things as necessary and to check back understanding.

Dyslexic students will have a particular difficulty with note-taking in lectures. You could help them by providing them in advance with an outline of your lecture, preferably on the college intranet, and by allowing them to tape the lecture. It would also be helpful to leave five minutes or so at the end of a lecture so that students, dyslexic or otherwise, can check with you any queries they have.

Writing

Dyslexic students are likely to make mistakes with spelling, punctuation and grammar and to have difficulty with the presentation of their work. So, as far as possible, rate their work on content rather than form. Also, be aware that students will be slow in doing written work, and consider extending deadlines for essays.

As noted above, it's important to be sure that students understand exactly what is required by an essay question. You could perhaps give them some help

Sylvia Moody, *Dyslexia: Surviving and succeeding at college* (Oxon: Routledge, 2007).

with structuring their essay; for example, you could ask them to make notes for their essay and then look over their notes with them. In general, students benefit very much from understanding how to structure their ideas; otherwise they tend to get lost in detail and lose the thread of their argument.

Organisation

Difficulties with structure impact on general organisational skills. So you could give students help with scheduling their work, e.g., helping them estimate how much time they need for researching, planning and writing an essay. Similarly, you could keep an eye on their general study and revision schedules.

Motor skills

Students with poor motor skills will probably have slow and untidy handwriting, so you could make allowances for this and allow them to type their work as far as possible. They may be able to get permission to use a word processor in their examinations.

If you have science students who have to do laboratory work which requires good manual skills, then you may need to observe how they are doing things and perhaps suggest better methods. If manual difficulties are causing a real problem, you could suggest a referral to an occupational therapist.

Sylvia Moody, *Dyslexia: Surviving and succeeding at college* (Oxon: Routledge, 2007).

Photocopiable
Resource

These, then, are some of the ways in which you could help dyslexic and dyspraxic students. In general, you need to strike a balance between giving students enough help to put them on a level playing field with their non-dyslexic peers but not so much help that they don't learn how to do things themselves. They need to become confident about working independently in preparation for moving on into employment, where they are unlikely to find the same level of support as they do at college.

Sylvia Moody, *Dyslexia: Surviving and succeeding at college* (Oxon: Routledge, 2007).

Chapter 12

Beyond college

The world of work

You may already have experience of the world of work, or you may be on the threshold of entering it. Whatever your situation, you will need to be aware of the ways in which your dyslexic or dyspraxic difficulties may affect your work performance and to know about the help and support which you are entitled to receive.

Career choice

If you are going to be entering employment for the first time after your years at college, you may well be considering what career path you want to follow and wondering whether some careers are more suited than others to a dyslexic person. There is no simple answer to this question. You have to balance a number of factors: what career actually interests you, what the demands of it are likely to be, and whether you feel that, with appropriate support, you will be able to cope reasonably well with those demands.

It's hard to decide theoretically if something is going to suit you or not, so, to some extent, your first job will be a trial run. However, there might be some obvious minefields. For example, if you're a very slow reader, you might think twice about training as a solicitor or barrister, professions in which you have to do large amounts of reading at short notice. If you are inaccurate with numbers, perhaps accountancy is not for you. If you're very slow with writing, journalism might be too much of a challenge. And if you have poor motor skills, perhaps joinery should not be your career of choice.

Also, beware of generalisations about what dyslexic people can and can't do. It is often assumed, for example, that dyslexic people have good visual skills and so will excel in professions such as design or architecture. However, as Clare pointed out in Chapter 10 (pp. 165–6), this is not necessarily the case. So, think realistically about what *your* skills are and what type of job you would feel comfortable in.

If there is a particular career path which you are really keen to follow, then it's probably a good idea to 'give it a go', if you possibly can, while always being aware that it might not work. They say it's best to regret what you've done rather than what you haven't done. But always have a Plan B.

Disclosing dyslexia to an employer

The next thing to think about, if you are applying for a job, is: are you going to tell your potential employer that you are dyslexic? Again, no simple answer. If your difficulties aren't severe and you don't believe they will affect your job, maybe you don't need to mention it. But then, can you know in advance exactly what the job will entail and how your difficulties might trip you up?

Another question is, if you do disclose your dyslexia, is it better to do this in your job application or interview, or wait until you are in post? Again, who can tell? It's a gamble. If you mention your dyslexia in your application, it could count against you. However, if you don't mention it at least in your interview, your employer would be under no obligation later to offer you support.

An advantage of disclosing your dyslexia at the application stage is that you can request some concessions in the application procedure. For example, you could ask for the application form to be e-mailed rather than posted to you. Then you can fill it in on your computer, which means you can redraft it as often as necessary and have the use of the spellchecker.

As regards the interview itself, you could ask for questions to be given to you in advance so that you could prepare your answers. Also, you could notify the interviewers beforehand that you might have some difficulty speaking impromptu and that you might need to have questions repeated.

If the application procedure includes a written test, you could ask for extra time for this or for the questions to be read out to you. Or, if the test does not reflect the work that would be done in your job, you could request that the test be waived altogether.

During your interview, the interview panel's perception of you is likely to be influenced by the *manner* in which you talk about your dyslexia. If you present it in too rosy a light, you might be dismissed as unrealistic. If you talk about it in a hesitant or furtive way, that will certainly count against you. But if you can talk about it in a sensible, matter-of-fact way – pointing out advantages and disadvantages and explaining how you have sought and profited from help – this could be very much in your favour.

Help and support in the work place

If, having disclosed your dyslexia, you accept a job offer, then your employer has a legal obligation to provide you with reasonable help and support. This should include arranging a workplace needs assessment and appropriate training, for which funds are available through the Access to Work scheme. The employer should also make reasonable adjustments in the workplace to accommodate your difficulties. Such adjustments could include:

- giving taped instructions to back up written ones;
- using voicemail rather than memos;
- giving IT support, e.g., speech-to-text, or text-to-speech software;
- allowing you extra time to complete tasks;
- providing a talking calculator;
- providing a voice recorder;
- helping you organise your work schedule;
- providing a quiet work space;
- allowing time off for dyslexia-specific training.

If you need further advice about your rights as a dyslexic employee, you could consult the Disability Rights Commission (p. 210) or the disability employment adviser at your local JobCentre Plus. For organisations that offer workplace needs assessments, workplace training and employment consultancy, see pp. 204–6.

Epilogue

I hope you have enjoyed this book and have found it useful.

If, having reached the end of the book, you can't remember much about what you've read, don't worry. There was a lot to take in. Just go back and take one chapter at a time, beginning with the chapters most relevant to your needs. Read each chapter through carefully, one section at a time, and work through any exercises given in the chapter. In particular, practice the note-taking techniques illustrated in Chapter 6.

You need *gradually* to take on board all the advice given. Keep the book handy so that you can dip into it at odd moments to refresh your memory about the strategies you can use to make life easier for yourself.

It remains only for me to wish you every success in your studies, and in your life beyond college.

Sylvia Moody

Part IV

Further help and advice

Introduction

In this last section of the book, you will find checklists on dyslexic and dyspraxic difficulties and on visual stress. There is also advice on IT support and other technological aids which you may find useful, a list of support organisations and suggestions for further reading.

Checklists

Tick the items that cause you difficulty. If you find you have ticked a lot of items, take further advice from the British Dyslexia Association (p. 202). You may like to consider having a formal assessment.

Dyslexic difficulties at college

Reading

Reading quickly .... ☐
Reading with good comprehension .... ☐
Learning from books.. ☐
Recalling what has been read.................................... ☐
Reading aloud... ☐

Writing

Writing neatly .... ☐
Writing quickly .... ☐
Writing reversible letters (b, d, p, g, m, w) .... ☐
Sequencing letters (was-saw)..................................... ☐

Spelling .... ☐
Putting ideas down in writing................................. ☐
Writing a cheque... ☐
Filling in forms.. ☐
Writing a letter .... ☐
Writing a report/essay.. ☐

Speech and comprehension

Saying long words.. ☐
Speaking in public .... ☐
Explaining things to people simply and clearly .... ☐
Following conversations or discussions...................... ☐
Taking notes at a lecture or meeting......................... ☐

Memory and concentration

Remembering and following instructions................... ☐
Remembering
  • messages... ☐
  • telephone numbers... ☐
  • times of seminars/lectures .... ☐
  • times of appointments .... ☐
Doing sums in your head... ☐
Concentrating for long periods .... ☐
Organising a study schedule/daily life .... ☐

Orientation

Following left/right instructions .... ☐
Reading maps .... ☐
Finding your way in a strange place .... ☐
Looking things up in dictionaries/directories .... ☐

Everyday difficulties

Writing a cheque .... ☐
Filling in forms .... ☐
Writing letters .... ☐
Reading letters .... ☐
Reading official documents .... ☐
Reading a newspaper .... ☐
Understanding operating/safety instructions on
　　household gadgets .... ☐
Reading television schedules .... ☐
Reading recipes .... ☐
Reading bus/train timetables .... ☐
Making shopping lists .... ☐
Dealing with money in shops .... ☐
Checking bank statements .... ☐
Keeping track of outstanding bills .... ☐
Explaining things clearly to others .... ☐
Placing orders over the telephone .... ☐
Conducting enquiries over the telephone .... ☐
Following spoken instructions .... ☐
Following left-right instructions .... ☐
Reading maps .... ☐
Reading signposts .... ☐

Orienting oneself in a strange place or complex
environment, e.g., tube station .... ☐
Remembering where things have been put .... ☐
Looking up telephone numbers in directories .... ☐
Recording telephone numbers correctly .... ☐
Remembering messages .... ☐
Remembering appointments .... ☐
Organising daily life .... ☐
Concentrating for longer than an hour .... ☐
Working continuously for longer than an hour .... ☐

Dyspraxia

Do you bump into things/people and often trip
over? .... ☐
Do you spill and drop things often? .... ☐
Do you find it difficult to do practical tasks such as:
- cooking .... ☐
- DIY .... ☐
- typing .... ☐
- keying numbers on the 'phone .... ☐
- driving a car .... ☐
- riding a bike .... ☐
Do you find sports difficult, especially team and bat
and ball games? .... ☐
Do you find it difficult to judge distance and
space? .... ☐
Are you over/undersensitive to:
- sound .... ☐
- smell .... ☐
- taste .... ☐

Are you generally disorganised and untidy? .... ☐
Do you have problems prioritising and
  discriminating the essential from the inessential? ☐
Do you find it hard to finish off work? .... ☐
Do you often lose things and find it difficult to
  remember where you have put them? .... ☐
Do you have problems working against a
  background of noise? .... ☐
Is there a delay between hearing something and
  understanding it? .... ☐
Do you take spoken and written words literally
  and find it hard to pick up shades of meaning? ...... ☐
Do you find it difficult to interpret body language? ... ☐
Do you interrupt people often? .... ☐

Visual stress

Do you find it hard to focus on written text? .... ☐
Does reading make you tired? .... ☐
Do you often lose your place when reading? .... ☐
Do you reread or skip lines when reading? .... ☐
Do you ever read words/numbers back to front? .... ☐
Do you miss out words when reading? .... ☐
Do you tend to misread words? .... ☐
Do you use a marker or your finger to keep the
  place? .... ☐
Are you easily distracted when reading? .... ☐
Do you become restless or fidgety when reading? ...... ☐
Do you get headaches when you read? .... ☐
Do your eyes become sore or water? .... ☐
Do you screw your eyes up when reading? .... ☐

Do you rub or close one eye when reading?............... ☐
Do you read close to the page? .... ☐
Do you push the page away?.. ☐
Do you prefer dim light to bright light for reading?.. ☐
Does white paper (or white board) seem to glare?..... ☐
Does it all become harder the longer you read?......... ☐
Does print become distorted as you read? .... ☐

Useful equipment

There is a wide range of IT equipment and other technological aids which are helpful to dyslexic and dyspraxic students. If you are in receipt of a Disabled Students Allowance, this allowance can be used to buy such equipment. The particular items of equipment which will be helpful to you will be identified in your Needs Assessment (see page 25). If you buy equipment yourself, consult a specialist in the field (see pages 207–8). Try to get a hands-on demonstration or a free trial of software before making a purchase.

Caution: If you already own a computer, don't purchase any software until you've checked with the supplier that it's compatible with your equipment.

You may be able to apply for VAT relief on certain items. For advice on this contact: iANSYST Ltd, tel. 0800 018 0045, e-mail reception@dyslexic.com.

Computer

When considering purchasing a new computer, think carefully before choosing between a desktop and a laptop. Laptops are easy to carry around, but they are easily damaged or stolen.

Computer accessories

A USB storage device ('thumb drive') allows you to carry copies of your computer files around with you. To access your data, simply plug the device into another computer.

Caution: Some systems do not allow external drives to be plugged in and read.

It is useful to purchase a docking station so that all external hardware (printer, scanner, mouse, keyboard) can be left in place, and be reconnected with a single USB plug.

If you find that working on a laptop causes strain or discomfort, consider buying an external full-sized keyboard and mouse. An ergonomic keyboard (designed for comfort and ease of use) is a wise investment as it encourages good posture. Dyspraxic people, in particular, often find this type of keyboard helpful.

Also useful is an A4 paperholder which allows you to keep any papers you are referring to in a vertical position parallel to the screen. Book holders are also available.

Good working practices

Don't sit with the laptop on your lap. Sit in a chair with your laptop on a table or other solid surface.

Choose a chair that supports your back.

Don't sit too close to the screen. If possible, have the screen at right angles to the light source.

Visual sensitivity

Microsoft Windows operating systems allow customisation of your computer with tools designed to help users with disabilities. For example, changing screen and font colours can reduce eye strain and prevent text from swimming on the page. These functions are, however, limited, and you may prefer to buy a specialised piece of software that can change all Windows colours, including the background colour, default text colour, menu background, text colour and toolbars. Similar software for web pages is also available. A screen reading ruler is also useful.

When reading books or papers, you could use coloured overlays or eye-level coloured reading rulers. (See pages 208–9.)

Organisation

A personal digital assistant (PDA) is a hand-sized organiser that works like a mini-computer. It can store your diary, set alarmed reminders for appointments, create 'to-do' lists, store pictures, record notes and messages, and store documents for reading and editing wherever you are. You can synchronise your PDA with your desktop or laptop to keep your diary and important files up-to-date.

Caution: Some PDAs have very limited memory, so will not store much data or many files.

Caution: Make sure that the PDA comes pre-loaded with the correct software you need to be able to read your files.

If you don't have a PDA, there are some useful tools available within Microsoft Office. Microsoft Outlook, for example, has a simple-to-use calendar/diary function with audible alarm.

Speech recognition

There are software packages that allow you to dictate into your computer and have the written word appear on the screen. The text can then be edited and printed, using, for example, Microsoft Word. The software also has the ability to transcribe your voice recordings from digital recorders and PDAs.

Text to speech

These programs can read out loud practically any text that is on the screen. Hearing what you have written read back to you often helps with proofing your work. Some programs can also read toolbars and drop-down menus.

Scanning

OCR (optical character recognition) software can scan printed documents and convert them into text documents on your computer. You can then read the document on your computer screen in the colour and format that suits you best: perhaps in larger print, with double spacing, or using different coloured backgrounds and print. Alternatively, you can use a scanner in conjunction with text to speech software to have the documents read aloud to you.

Caution: Scanning whole books or large amounts of text is laborious and may often not be worth the effort.

Note-taking

You can use a digital voice recorder to 'jot down' notes and reminders to yourself. Depending on the quality of the recordings, these 'notes' can be transcribed by Dragon speech-recognition (PC only) into a word-processing package.

Caution: Make sure you choose a recorder that has a long recording time and PC connectivity.

The recorder can also be used to record lectures, tutorials and meetings for playing back at a later time, reducing the need to take hand-written notes. Recording efficiency varies according to the acoustic environment. It is usually preferable to use an external microphone.

Caution: Speech-recognition software is trained to understand *your* voice, so it will *not* be able to transcribe recordings of lectures and seminars.

Typing tutors

Being able to type confidently, accurately and quickly will free up your mind to concentrate on the content of what you are typing. There are several computer-interactive typing tutors which will give you training in touch-typing.

Spelling

Make sure you are making the best use of the spell checkers that come as standard in, for example, Microsoft Office. There are also sophisticated add-ons to word processing packages that offer phonetic and homophone spell checkers, and word prediction. Hand-held spell-checkers are also available.

Structuring written work

You can plan and structure essays and reports using computer generated spider maps, flow charts, etc. At the click of your mouse these can then be converted into text and exported to your preferred word-processing package, presentation software (such as Powerpoint) or other software packages.

Giving talks/presentations

It is helpful if tutors use an 'interactive' whiteboard, linked to a computer. They can then:

- write on the screen to highlight and annotate points in documents and presentations;
- view and navigate the internet and display websites which the whole audience will be able to see;
- project movie files and DVDs onto a large screen;
- allow members of the audience to add their contributions to word processing documents, spreadsheets, etc., by writing directly onto them;
- save the information for printing off as handout notes, or uploading onto the internet/intranet.

Whiteboard 'glare' can be avoided by changing the colours projected onto the screen through the computer's Windows properties/appearance function.

Route planning and navigation systems

Route planners are computer programs displaying street maps and road networks throughout the UK and abroad. They enable you to plot the route to your destination, and can be accessed through a website, your desktop PC, laptop, or PDA. Most systems let you print out maps of the proposed route as well as directions, such as when to take a turn.

Navigation systems are linked to the global positioning system (GPS), which uses satellites to locate your position anywhere in the world to within a few metres. The software can direct you along a route as you travel, whether you are walking or driving. All these systems have visual instructions; some also give spoken directions.

Caution: Take care to choose the style of interface that suits you best. Some people prefer detailed maps, others simple directional arrows.

Useful addresses

Help and advice organisations

For students

SKILL: National Bureau for Students with Disabilities

Chapter House, 18–20 Crucifix Lane, London SEI 3JW, UK
Tel: 020 7450 0620
E-mail: skill@skill.org.uk
Web site: www.skill.org.uk

World of Dyslexia Ltd

Web site: www.dyslexia-college.com
Offers useful information on topics from reading techniques to applying for grants.

General

Bangor Dyslexia Unit

University of Wales, Gwynedd LL57 2DG, UK
Tel: 01248 382 203

E-mail: dyslex-admin@bangor.ac.uk
Web site: www.dyslexia.bangor.ac.uk
This branch covers the whole of Wales.

British Dyslexia Association
98 London Road, Reading, Berks RG1 5AU, UK
Tel: 0990 134 248 or 01189 668 271
E-mail: helpline@bdadyslexia.org.uk
Web site: www.bdadyslexia.org.uk
For list of all local associations, click on 'Information'
on home page.

Dyslexia Association of Ireland
1 Suffolk Street, Dublin 2, Ireland
Tel: (+353 1) 1679 0276
E-mail: info@dyslexia-ie
Web site: www.dyslexia.ie

Dyslexia Association of London
Dyslexia Resource Centre, The Munro Centre,
66 Snowsfields, London SE1 3SS, UK
Tel: 020 8788 0900
E-mail: dal1449@btconnect.com
Web site: www.dyslexiainlondon.ik.com

Dyslexia in Scotland
Stirling Business Centre, Wellgreen, Stirling FK8 2DZ,
UK
Tel: 01786 446650
E-mail: info@dyslexia-in-scotland.org
Web site: www.dyslexia.scotland.dial.pipex.com

European Dyslexia Association

E-mail: eda@kbnet.co.uk
Web site: www.dyslexia.eu.com

International Dyslexia Association

Web site: www.interdys.org

Dyslexia assessment and tuition

It is important that assessment and tuition are carried
out by chartered psychologists or teachers who are
dyslexia specialists and have experience in working
with adults. Your college should be able to make
recommendations. Otherwise, consult your local branch
of the British Dyslexia Association (see above) or
Dyslexia Action (see below) for advice.

Assessment for adults

Dyslexia Action

Park House, Wick Road, Egham, Surrey TW20 0HH,
UK
Tel: 01784 222 300
E-mail: info@dyslexiaaction.org.uk
Web site: www.dyslexiaaction.org.uk

Dyslexia Assessment Service

22 Wray Crescent, London N4 3LP, UK
Tel: 020 7272 6429

Dyslexia Teaching Centre
23 Kensington Square, London W8 5HN, UK
Tel: 020 7361 4790
E-mail: dyslexiateacher@tiscali.co.uk
Web site: www.dyslexia-teaching-centre.org.uk

Helen Arkell Dyslexia Centre
Frensham, Farnham, Surrey GU10 3BW, UK
Tel: 01252 792 400
E-mail: enquiries@arkellcentre.org.uk
Web site: www.arkellcentre.org.uk
Covers Surrey, Hampshire, south-west London.

London Dyslexia Action
2 Grosvenor Gardens, London SW1W 0DH, UK
Tel: 020 7730 8890
E-mail: london@dyslexiaaction.org.uk
Web site: www.dyslexiaaction.org.uk

PATOSS (dyslexia tutors organisation)
PO Box 10, Evesham, Worcestershire WR11 6ZW, UK
Tel: 01386 712650
E-mail: patoss@evesham.ac.uk
Web site: www.patoss-dyslexia.org

Workplace dyslexia specialists

Dyslexia Advice and Training Services
33 South Grove House, London N6 6LR, UK
Tel: 020 8348 7110
E-mail: brianhagan2003@yahoo.co.uk

Dyslexia Assessment and Consultancy
39 Cardigan Street, Kennington, London SE11 5PF, UK
Tel: 020 8883 1753
Fax: 020 7587 0546
E-mail: info@workingwithdyslexia.com
Web site: www.workingwithdyslexia.com

Dyslexia Assessment Service
22 Wray Crescent, London N4 3LP, UK
Tel: 020 7272 6429

Dyslexia Consultancy
6 Gilbert Road, Malvern, Worcestershire WR14 3RQ,
UK
Tel: 01684 572 466
E-mail: dyslexia.mj@dsl.pipex.com

Fitzgibbon Associates
39–41 North Road, London N7 9DP, UK
Tel: 020 7609 7809
E-mail: fae@fitzgibbonassociates.co.uk

Independent Dyslexia Consultants
1–7 Woburn Walk, London WC1H 0JJ, UK
Tel: 020 7383 3724
E-mail: info@dyslexia-idc.org

Key4Learning
The Old Village Stores, Cheap Street, Chedworth,
Gloucester GL54 4AA, UK
Tel: 01285 720 964
Web site: www.key4learning.com

Workplace advice

Access to Work Business Centres
See telephone directory for local centre.

Dyslexia Adults link
Web site: www.dyslexia-adults.com
Offers general advice for adult dyslexics and has an extensive section on workplace difficulties.

Jobcentre Plus
Web site: www.jobcentre.plus.gov.uk/cms.asp
Offers advice on coping with disability in the workplace.

Working with Dyslexia
Web site: www.workingwithdyslexia.com/
info-sheets.php

Dyspraxia support

Developmental Adult Neuro-Diversity Association (DANDA)
46 Westbere Road, London NW2 3RU, UK
Tel: 020 7435 7891
E-mail: mary@pmcolley.freeserve.co.uk
Web site: www.danda.org.uk

Dyscovery Centre
4a Church Road, Whitchurch, Cardiff CF14 2DZ, UK
Tel: 02920 628 222
E-mail: info@dyscovery.co.uk
Web site: www.dyscovery.co.uk

Dyspraxia Association of Ireland
c/o Chestnut View, Ryevale Lawns, Leixlip,
Co. Kildare, Ireland
Tel: 01 295 7125
E-mail: dyspraxiaireland@eircomnet
Web site: www.dyspraxiaireland.com

Dyspraxia Connexion
Web site: www. dysf.fsnet.co.uk

Dyspraxia Foundation
8 West Alley, Hitchin, Hertfordshire SG5 1EG, UK
Tel: 01462 454986
E-mail: admin@dyspraxiafoundation.org.uk
Web site: www.dyspraxiafoundation.org.uk

Helpful gadgets

Disabled Living Foundation
Tel: 0845 130 9177
Web site: www.dlf.org.uk

IT advice and training

AbilityNet
PO Box 94, Warwick CV34 5WS, UK
Tel: 01926 312847 or 0800 269545 (helpline freephone)
E-mail: enquiries@abilitynet.org.uk
Web site: www.abilitynet.org.uk

Dyslexia in the Workplace
Flat 2, Grafton Chambers, Churchway, London NW1 1LN, UK
Tel: 020 7388 3807
E-mail: workplacedyslexia@btopenworld.com

Iansyst Training Project
Fen House, Fen Road, Cambridge CB4 1UN, UK
Tel: 01223 420101
E-mail: reception@dyslexic.com
Web site: www.dyslexic.com

Local consultant
To find a local consultant, check with your local branch of the British Dyslexia Association (see above).

Visual problems: colorimetry assessment

Colorimetry assessments are not done in standard eye tests; contact the Dyslexia Research Trust or Cerium Visual Technologies (below) for a specialist in your area.

Barnard Associates

58 Clifton Gardens, London NW11 7EL, UK
Tel: 020 8458 0599
E-mail: sb@eye-spy.co.uk

Cerium Visual Technologies

Tenterden, Kent TN30 7DE, UK
Tel: 01580 765 211
E-mail: ceriumuk@ceriumvistech.co.uk
Web site: www.ceriumvistech.co.uk
Manufactures tinted overlays.

Crossbow Education

Web site: www.crossboweducation.com
Supplies screen reading rulers.

Dyslexia Research Trust

University Laboratory of Physiology, Oxford OX1 3PT,
UK
Tel: 01865 272 500
E-mail: info@dyslexic.org.uk
Web site: www.dyslexic.org.uk

Institute of Optometry

56–62 Newington Causeway, London SE1 6DS, UK
Tel: 020 7234 9641
E-mail: admin@ioo.org.uk
Web site: www.ioo.org.uk

Audio libraries

Calibre
Web site: www.calibre.org.uk

Listening Books
Web site: www.listening-books.org.uk

Legal advice

Disability Rights Commission
Web site: www.drc-gb.org

General counselling

Student health centre
Counsellors will be available at the student health centre at your college.

British Association of Counselling and Psychotherapy
BACP House, 15 St John's Business Park, Lutterworth, LE17 4HB, UK
Tel: 0870 443 5252
Web site: www.bacp.co.uk

Further reading

General interest

The Adult Dyslexic: Interventions and Outcomes, David McLoughlin, Carol Leather, Patricia Stringer (London: Whurr Publishers, 2002).

Dyslexia and Stress, ed. Tim Miles (London: Whurr Publishers, 2004).

The Dyslexic Adult in a Non-Dyslexic World, Ellen Morgan and Cynthia Klein (London: Whurr Publishers, 2000).

Making Dyslexia Work for You: A Self-help Guide, Vicki Goodwin and Bonita Thomson (London: David Fulton, 2004).

For students

Dyslexia at College, Tim Miles and Dorothy Gilroy (London and New York: Routledge, 1995).

Use Your Head, Tony Buzan (London: BBC Books, 2003).

Dyslexia: A Teenager's Guide, Sylvia Moody (London: Vermilion, 2004).

For people in employment

Dyslexia in the Workplace, Diana Bartlett and Sylvia Moody (London: Whurr Publishers, 2000).

Dyslexia in Adults: Education and Employment, Gavin Reid and Jane Kirk (London: Wiley, 2001).

Adult Dyslexia: A Guide for the Workplace, Gary Fitzgibbon and Brian O'Connor (London: Wiley, 2002).

Dyslexia: How to Survive and Succeed at Work, Sylvia Moody (London: Vermilion, 2006).

For employers

Briefing Paper 6 on Dyslexia in the Workplace. Available from Employers Forum on Disability, Tel: 020 7403 3020, e-mail: www.employers-forum.co.uk.

For unions

Dyslexia in the Workplace: A Guide for Unions. Brian Hagan. Available from the TUC.

For teachers

Dyslexia in Secondary School, Jenny Cogan and Mary Flecker (London: Whurr Publishers, 2004).

Dyslexia and the Curriculum. A series of books covering individual GCSE subjects (London: British Dyslexia Association/David Fulton, 2003, ongoing).

Dyspraxia

Living with Dyspraxia, ed. Mary Colley (London: Jessica Kingsley, 2004).

Index